T0194672

Cool Memories IV

Cool Memories IV
1995–2000

Jean Baudrillard

Translated by Chris Turner

VERSO

London • New York

This edition first published by Verso 2003
© Verso 2003
Translation © Chris Turner 2003

First published as *Cool Memories IV 1995‑2000*
© Editions Galilée 2000
All rights reserved

1 3 5 7 9 10 8 6 4 2

Verso
UK: 6 Meard Street, London W1F 0EG
USA: 388 Atlantic Ave, NY 11217
www.versobooks.com

Verso is the imprint of New Left Books

ISBN 1–85984–535–5
ISBN 1–85984–462–6 (pbk)

British Library Cataloguing in Publication Data
A catalogue record for this book is available from the British Library

Library of Congress Cataloging-in-Publication Data
A catalog record for this book is available from the Library of Congress

Typeset in Bembo by M Rules
Printed in the United States

Very Zarathustrian, this silent laughter. Flowers laugh silently. Grass and plants and the whole forest laugh silently. The sky and the stars laugh silently. If there is a background noise to the universe, it is this silent laughter, this inaudible sound like a distant echo of man's emergence and the catastrophe of the real world.

The line where the waters divide – the line where thoughts divide. No planispheric extension. Waters and destinies always divide.

There is a magnetic pole of invisible events (different from the pole of history) which, by their mass, deflect the trajectory of historical events.

There is also a curvature, similar to that of the earth and of physical space, to mental space and historical space, which renders unthinkable any idea of planning and linearity.

An isothermal world, with no evaporation because there is no wind and no sun, is a dead world. Similarly, a body in which, by containment of its fluids, nothing evaporates any longer, from which no secretion emanates – as in today's radical sanitarianism – is a dead body.

Victims of all countries, beware of avenging yourselves. You would no longer deserve our pity. Do not let vengeance erase the horror of the massacre.

Just one person too many, and everywhere a throng.[1]

The concept is unrepresentable, but the image is inexplicable. Between them there is, then, an insuperable distance. As a result, the image is always nostalgic for the text and the text nostalgic for the image.

You have to live in collusion with the system and in revolt against its consequences. You have to live with the idea that we have survived the worst.

We have to take the view that we have entered a phase of thought-prohibition, and

---

1. 'Un seul être de trop, et tout est surpeuplé'. Baudrillard is playing here on Lamartine's line 'Un seul être vous manque et tout est dépeuplé' (*Méditations*). This line was famously parodied by Jean Giraudoux, the author of *La Guerre de Troie n'aura pas lieu*: 'Un seul être vous manque et tout est repeuplé.' [This note and all subsequent notes are mine. – *Trans.*]

so we must prepare to go underground, to take refuge in the catacombs of the Virtual.

A simple glance around the political scene tells us just how insignificant it is. But power remains, as hygienic, therapeutic function, as apotropaic rite,[2] as antidepressant.

Spells of time hang over the numerical extension of time like patches of territory over the full extension of the map, like scraps of writing wrenched from the servitude of language, like scraps of images wrenched from the increasingly spectral self-evidence of reality.

Cynicism goes well with *le canicule* – the heat-wave – as it does also with 'a dog's life'.[3] The ego wavers in the heat-wave, but the superego functions better, moving in the ice-cold space of the will.

Those shoulders I discovered against the whiteness of a hospital bed and which I found again, just as stunning, in the black sheath of a wedding dress.

Salieri is absolutely right: perfection and grace (that of Mozart) are criminal, and

2. A rite averting evil.
3. The term cynic derives from the Greek *kune*, a dog.

must be destroyed. This insult to universal mediocrity must be avenged. Salieri's is a cry of protest against the inequality of destinies we suffer. But democratic redemption is just as unacceptable.

That divine mercy is infinite merely means that it is an infinite distance away (Updike).

By contrast with the beating of a butterfly's wings which ends in a whirlwind on the other side of the world, can we not imagine a hurricane which would end in the beating of a butterfly's wings? Or a light breeze which would end, on the other side of the world, in a cataclysm of butterfly's wings? In the end, perhaps chaos theory applies only to hurricanes and butterflies?

Detecting the background noise of the philosophical universe. Which leaves Marx's theory making noise again in cyberspace. Though scarcely audible, it tells us how many light-years we are from the revolution – the inaugural historical event which, like the Big Bang or the primal crime, never actually took place, and which it is absolutely impossible for us ever to approach. As a result, no historical truth is possible, nor any science of origins.

The strange dream of a penis penetrating the meatus of another male organ, which itself becomes confused with a female sex organ (in the dream, all this seems entirely plausible). In the end, they are two Siamese twins joined by a single convergent penis, like a Klein bottle, that topological figure in which the neck folds back round into the base, forming a single convex object.

Whereas the two were once happy or unhappy together, now the one automatically feels better when the other feels worse. This balance can be maintained indefinitely. In the perfect couple, what disappears in the one reappears in the other.

When a woman says: I want to make love with you, it is an offer. When a man says it, it is a request. The absolute priority of offer over request, supply over demand. But when a woman offers herself, it is always also a request (for assent), and when a man requests that she offer herself, he makes her an offer of his request.

The finest crime story.

By piling up the evidence, the murderer succeeds in convincing his friend that it was he who committed the murder, while sleepwalking. The friend is found guilty and serves his sentence under the mistaken impression that he was the murderer. Twenty years later they meet again and the real killer, providing proof, on this occasion, of his friend's innocence, in a sense completes his murder by this murderous revelation. In a sudden blinding flash – but too late – the friend divines that the other man was responsible for the whole thing. Esoteric criminology, as Ceronetti would say.

Thought and reality are moving apart from each other at considerable speed in a divergent, strabismic movement. Thought squints out at its unfathomable perplexity, and reality is becoming increasingly murky [*louche*].[4]

4. There is a play here on the French words '*louche*' and '*loucher*' (to squint).

The system and the analysis are like rival shadows. The more the one becomes optimized, the more the other is radicalized. But who cares about this radicalism now? It is no longer revulsive, but laxative. You think you are the Exterminating Angel, but you are merely the clyster!

The wicked pleasure, even though standards have fallen very low, of seeing people compete to go even lower. Intellectual cowardice has become the true Olympic discipline of our time. A brutish consensus is being struck on the lowest common denominator.

Over the years, the Beautiful, the Good and the True have played out a strange game of musical chairs. In the beginning, Good and moral values reign supreme. But then Evil assumes an aesthetic value: ugliness becomes beautiful. This is all swept away by the Real which, being neither beautiful nor ugly, becomes true. Objectivity becomes the dominant moral value. But not for long, for in the end the simulacrum and the Virtual win out over all values.

The hypothesis (in quantum physics) of the inseparability of 'twin' particles is currently being verified in the global simultaneity of news and information – with all the points of the globe crowded together in real time, with space and time abolished. Only that simultaneity is combined with an irremediable separation of things from each other. The mental crowding is accompanied by an insuperable distance between bodies.

What is consoling, as we grow old, is that the current world is ageing more quickly than we are. At this rate, we shall outlive it.

The prison house at Ushuaia, the jail of the *Recidivistas*. The prisoner of whom we know nothing – neither his name, his crime, his ultimate destiny nor the date of his death. But a photo still remains of him – a single photo. The brother in captivity of all those Indians whose names and crimes we also do not know, but whose ultimate destiny we know only too well.

A strange world of criminals, exiles, anarchists (including the one who blew up the Buenos Aires police chief and was pardoned after twenty years and sent into exile), Indians, Salesian missionaries, charitable parasites of this ill-starred land, which they evangelize like the lichen that wraps itself around the forests of nothofagus and submerges those trees as they submit to its phagacytosis.

Devastated forests seemingly felled by some recent cataclysm. Hulks of wrecked ships. Graveyards of immigrants and sailors. And today the disaster of an anachronistic modernity: concrete, dust, traffic, engine noise – a sacrilege, as though the silence of the ends of the earth had to be obliterated.

You think you have left the world behind, but with its faxes, technology, motorcycles, videos and duty-frees, it got here before you. To come here is to dream of a possible end of all things – and of thought. But we confirm here that the world's only extremity is the extremity of endless circulation. Wherever you are, you are hostage to the global network. It is impossible to cut the umbilical cord. You are yourself an extreme phenomenon, gone beyond your own end.

The Alakaluf did not know they were at the ends of the earth. The Indians of Tierra del Fuego were where they were and nowhere else. The sailors, adventurers, missionaries and outlaws also discovered, in their time, another world entirely unlike their own. We, by contrast, are here as tourists, with our pride at having discovered everything, and our regret at a finite world.

A devastated universe and, at the same time, a sense of archaic dereliction. An earlier disaster, reaching back into the depths of time, but one that is still going on. A sense of accursedness which the Fuegians transposed on to their own gods when they had any – it was difficult for gods to get a foothold in a world without sun or pity, not even the pity of the elements one for another. Neither traces of human beings, nor the natural grandeur of a desert: wherever you go in Patagonia, you find the opposite of nature, and of culture. The immensity of a territory without relief, the nullity of a sterile horizon, a diluvian or antediluvian form. Neither towns nor landscapes – these things have meaning only in a civilized world. The 'urban' zones are a wasteland of dust, concrete and neon, of artificial noise and musical, sartorial, mechanical and technical vulgarity.

Here, all that is inhuman is sublime, all that is human is squalid. Being 'at the ends of the earth' highlights this contrast. What you find there is not an original world, but the mix of an indestructible, wild form and the equally destructive grasp of the human species.

Immediately after: New York. Tierra del Fuego being the distant, peripheral extremity, New York the central extremity, the extreme centre of gravity of our world. Each, in its way, gives the impression of being on another planet. The dilation of geological time on Tierra del Fuego; here its diffraction and acceleration in real time – as timeless in its superficiality as the other in its depth. And if, down there, the sun lies to the north at noon, which always seems so marvellous to a northerner, it seems just as strange that the same sun rises and sets on New York, whose astral theme seems so indifferent to any other orbit but its own. Standing at the tip of Manhattan, towards Ellis and Staten Islands, you are on the banks of the Beagle Channel.

High tension – a perpetual anticyclone: since energy is a form of catastrophe, New York is indeed the epicentre of a catastrophe. The millions of people in the streets seem to have nothing to do but make New York exist – New York having nothing to do but be the centre of the world. It is in this sense that it represents only itself, and everything which happens here has global importance. It is the charm of this city to have turned not just the rest of the United States, but the rest of the world, into an immense province. Hence the foreboding of catastrophe which hovers over the whole city, though it is an exhilarated sense of foreboding, the sense of a collective sacrifice. No social bond, no conviviality, no responsibility to past or future – you don't reproduce in New York. New York isn't a city for reproducing in. Everything produces itself (everything happens) there, and that is that. It is a once-and-for-all city, with no thought for the morrow.

But when you go from Tierra del Fuego to Times Square, you cannot but be terrified by the proliferation of the human race. And you are compelled to think, like Ishi amid the crowds of San Francisco, that all the dead are present alongside the living, since there couldn't possibly be so many living people there at once: God could not watch over so many existences. Ten dead people for every living one seems a good proportion. As in the primal forest, for example, where there is one living tree to every ten dead ones. That's how it is, and it's no good getting too worked up about it. The conclusion is that, in this state of urban overpopulation, nine out of ten human beings are virtual corpses (even if outward appearances are deceptive); in other words, they are beings cut off from one another. Only a few thousand perhaps, in the best of cases, maintain a secret bond, and form a living symbolic chain, the only significant sequence in this immense, incapacitated human genome.

On Fifth Avenue a frail woman's body, in every way a symbol of the activist's defiance, brandishes a poster stigmatizing the prevalence of pornography. She brandishes it like her own identity photo. She is saying: Look who I am, look at this picture! as she pines away beneath the indifferent gaze of the crowd — a fine example of buckshee prostitution: the oldest profession in the world and the profession of faith intermingled beneath the banner of the Salvation Army.

   She has not understood that you should never hold up the mirror of their obscenity to people. If anything, they tend to regard themselves in it with pleasure. For this fatal error, this proselytical virgin would herself have deserved to be seduced, if not indeed piously debauched, with all the regard due to the femininity she was unwittingly flouting.

What does the fly understand of the window pane it bumps up against till it reaches the point of exhaustion? Nothing in nature offers any such obstacle to its natural instinct as this: a transparent one. We know no more of the transparent void which separates us from others than the fly knows of the insuperable obstacle of that glass surface.

Canetti: 'Whenever a truth threatens, man hides behind a thought.' Yes, but also: whenever a thought threatens, man hides behind the truth. He says: I don't mind being responsible for being, but not for appearances.

The mysteries of quantum physics: how does a particle disappear? We are told that it lasts for $1^{(-10)}$ seconds – but what becomes of it, since it is 'elementary'? And before it appears – it and its antiparticle – what was there? All these questions boil down to one: what is the world like when we are not there; what will it be like when we are no longer there? What did we do to appear, what shall we do to disappear? And what can the effect of our absence be? To know more, one has to use one's grey anti-matter. One has, as Canetti says, to have in oneself what might be called a mortal confidence.

Snowstorm. My flight is cancelled, so I won't make the appointment. But I am there all the same, since I should be, and everyone is expecting me. You can generalize this type of unforeseeable self-removal – it provides breathing space, charm, irony and depth. In fact, there is nothing more banal than being where you should be. Particularly if you are indispensable. There is nothing more petty than being where you are indispensable.

That which, in the untimely shadows, takes the form of a cerebral switching, to end in abandoning itself to the true god, who is the god of sleep.

Disappearance of the object into its system
Disappearance of production into its mirror
Disappearance of the real into the simulacrum
Disappearance of the Other into its double
Disappearance of the majorities into their silence
Disappearance of Evil into its transparency
Disappearance of seduction into the orgy
Disappearance of crime into its perfection
Disappearance of memory into commemoration
Disappearance of illusion into its end and, finally,
Disappearance of the illusionist himself, on stage, in the full glare of the lights. The illusionist, having displayed all his art, cannot but make himself disappear (without knowing how).

A change in the speaking style of announcers. The plummy voices of yesteryear maintained a steady crescendo right up to the end of the sentence. Today, the sentence is suspended before its end in a kind of apnoea, of artificial breathing, of inner gasping for breath, mimicking a searching for words which would seem to reflect thinking. All done to give a sense of the interactive truth of dialogue. In the past there was a theatrical staging of message, feeling and truth. Today the obscure genesis of speech is mimicked. Perhaps – who knows? – presenters also have an Unconscious, and their calculated hesitations are the reflection – there's no escaping psychoanalysis here – of the 'absence' of the Other. Rhetoric of the *Zeitgeist*.

. . . Abbey. Pink Chasubles Sunday.

We remain standing for the elevation of the host amid the prostrate worshippers. For this same reason – for not bowing when a procession passed by – the Chevalier de la Barre died at the stake. Times have indeed changed.

Executed at the age of twenty-seven. His effigy still stands in a recess, decorating a street corner at Gruissan. Washed-out colours, faded flowers. Behind the bars, the effigy itself remains a prisoner of intolerance.

Not to bow the head. A noble gesture, better than violence, better than armed revolt. In its elegance it is the purest, most radical act. Not to turn one's act into a moral cause, nor give one's gesture a universal meaning – simply not to bow the head. What act could match it today?

Today I can remain standing during the elevation, affront the host and its exposition with my gaze, without incurring any penalty whatever. Such is our freedom. But is this anything to be proud of?

In the modern abbey – all concrete and abstract stained-glass windows, with Christ as neo-Giottesque trapeze-artist above the empty altar – there reigns a flagrant absence of divinity. The miracle of the Incarnation is succeeded by the scandal of Disincarnation. Gregorian chants for the country retreat. The sermon on St John interviewing Christ: Are you the true Messiah, or must we await another?

(Christ's – apocryphal – reply: I am the true Messiah, but you mustn't tell anyone.) A few miles away, Stone Age Celtic gathering at the burial mound, eyes closed as a mark of silent synergy.

Clint Eastwood and *The Bridges of Madison County*.

Initially a cowboy-film hero, abstract and fleshless, asexual. Then an urban lawman, equally austere. A battler against evil, but with a certain weakness for the weaker sex. Ending up as a photographer. Still an outsider, but this time finding love in the clandestine intimacy of the rural world. The fine nostalgic coherence of an outsider, and one who will go back whence he came, but not before passing through all the mythological variants of his age, and of the cinema itself. The other tycoons (Brando, Nicholson) are monsters who don a different mask with every film and dissolve into the larger-than-life characters they play. Polymorphous monsters, whom a certain madness carries beyond their character parts, but who do not chart an individual course (not everyone has the good fortune to gamble his destiny on a single throw, like James Dean). Clint Eastwood is the only one to remain true to his mythological profile.

The airy utopia of strike days. Walking, walking, deprived, at last, of means of communication; deprived, at last, of one of life's conveniences for which we give nothing in return. A moment of withdrawal, a moment of perfection.

Catching the TGV just before the strike spreads to the whole network. No passengers (or hardly any), no ticket-inspectors, and perhaps even no driver. The image of an ideal society – a skeleton service on automatic pilot. A society of conditioned reflexes and invisible controls – perfect!

Scrutinizing people with such attention that they are forced to tell all.
Staring at people with such inattention that they are forced to remain silent.

Never do today what you could do only tomorrow. Since what you could do only tomorrow, you cannot do today. Never do in this life what you could do in another. Think of all those things which lost their charm because you had done them in a past life!

The idea of praying for souls in Purgatory is not a bad one. But, in the end, who are you praying for? For it's clear that we are in Purgatory, that we are serving our sentences there, and that even if we are redeemed by the death of Christ, we still have to slave for an eternity to pay off the interest. In fact we would do better to pray for the souls in Purgatory to stay where they are, since we know what Hell is like, and those burning there, since Hell is not being able ever to do anything but evil. But what about those who, in Paradise, will no longer have any idea of Evil? God alone knows what awaits them.

Anyway, Hell is unthinkable today. The perpetuity of Evil is unthinkable. Everything is against it – heredity, environment, the unconscious. Even past crimes are attenuating circumstances. Everything has become an attenuating circumstance through the interaction of culprit and victim, of genes and the will, of effect and cause.

Any form of thought whatever requires a preparation by emptying one's mind. You have to lance the cumulative abscess, since we know too much about everything. And there is nothing better than mindless diversions to rid us of that deadweight that crushes thought. Nothing like a good bout of obsessive gymnastics to dispel received ideas. The preparatives for thought are as mysterious as the preparatives for anger.

The reign of speculative stupidity, of statistical stupidity ('A majority of the French think that . . .'; '66 per cent believe Clinton is not in the wrong morally'), of expert language ('a major earthquake is expected in California within the next twenty years'; 'experts say there will be economic recovery in the autumn'), of flagrant disinformation ('the theory of terrorist action has been ruled out'), of the blatantly obvious ('the good weather has increased the risk of avalanches'). All news coverage is a speculation on credulity and stupidity.

Every day sees the miracle of the liquefaction of blood. The coagulated blood of the event flows out through the open wound of news coverage. Every day, our blood – after rising, by capillary action, into all the networks – liquefies in the newspapers and streams down the screens, as the blood of St Januarius does at set dates.

The ideal couple (Amélie Nothomb, *The Stranger Next Door*) is too good to be true. But the monstrous, bestial, obese and sexless couple is also too ugly to be true – gloomy ectoplasms of a radiant juvenility. The only truth lies in the combination of the two, given that each is the truth of the other. This is not so much evil as the truth of good but, rather, good as the hidden truth of evil. The spectre of good collaborating with the spectre of evil in the most total immorality. And Amélie's writing itself is, by its perfidiousness, party to this hypothesis.

The woman in a vegetative state raped at Rochester hospital (unhappy sister of the Marquise von O., romantically raped in her swoon), made pregnant and delivered – involuntarily, unconsciously and desirelessly – of a child she will never see. A symbol of the condition of all of us, mentally raped as we have been in our hypnotic state of politically decerebrated modern citizens, and left pregnant – virtually posthumously – with creatures we shall never know.

Being unable to prevent catastrophes, we have invented 'trauma counselling', in which we entrust the psychological monitoring of traumatized populations to experts. We mentally 'soundproof' the shock, so to speak, just as we soundproof events in the media by prohibiting the use of the images, just as we put prisoners into sensory deprivation in modern jails. No need to change life any longer, it is enough simply to act on the nerve endings or the screen of the brain.

Médecins sans frontières, journalists *sans frontières*, intellectuals *sans frontières* – this is the very leitmotiv of globalization: markets, information, pollution, corruption – all without frontiers. We would do better to seek frontiers for medicine, journalism and information. Even for culture, and for the universal in general.

A large part of contemporary writing, both novels and theory, has become user-friendly. It works as an all-inclusive package, references and allusions supplied, the whole thing ready-to-go, with the message thrown in as a bonus. It has given up its pact with the reader, given up that 'exotic' complicity which depends on an acute sense of distance, separation, severance, 'a dam which stops up the river of consciousness to raise its level, intensify its force and build its energy. . . .' Collusion with the reader is merely the product of facility.

To an objection about the simulacrum, he replies: Of course that doesn't stop this table existing materially! And he bangs his hand down on the table to prove his point. The trick had always worked before. But suddenly, one day, his hand goes right through. His audience collapse in laughter. You see, we told you he was just a conjurer!

Just as the scorpion threatened by fire shoots its own venom into itself, democracy encircled by the flames of free-market economics and the new world order pumps the searing venom of corruption into its veins. Thought, too, encircled by this gloomy reality, prefers to commit suicide by swallowing its own concept.

Exhibitions, museums, events: you are taken with the spectacle of the spectators much more than with what is to be seen or heard. And this makes it almost impossible to enjoy places and art, as the enormous meaninglessness of the crowd is against you – a meaninglessness that is considerably more significant, but signifying what?

The lecture: what am I doing here? But above all: what are they doing here – so many people gathered into a wide-eyed, open-mouthed, consenting mass? What induces them to take the dead man's place in this way (why is it so difficult for them to speak for themselves)? Yet a troubling impression, also, that they are going to devour you – and this may well be their secret desire. In fact they do not. They allow themselves to be lulled by the words, in a kind of silent convulsion or nervous lethargy. A similar fate befalls the hotel pianist: you notice his presence only when he stops playing, at which point automatic applause breaks out. Only once did they forget to applaud. They hadn't realized it was over.

The strange ballet performed by those who, passing on the same pavement, hurtle towards each other, and just miss a collision by inches.

There is the same scenario in stammering, where the words bump into each other as they come out – perhaps because, against the will of the speaker, they attract each other; or because he panics at these words coming out of him like things.

The advert featuring a young African woman – her features drawn, famished and ravaged by poverty. And the same woman again, who (thanks to your generous donation to the international aid organization) has now been restored to her radiant self, looking almost like a supermodel. So the woman who posed for the photo had to be extravagantly made over to look wretched. This is enough to cast doubt on any image – to make even the truth of poverty seem suspect. So the (unintended) message is that of the hypocrisy of a (humanitarian) movement capable of such media fakery. Deterrent advertising which turns us all to denial. The effort to publicize the truth leads to the denial of truth itself. Through an image strategy, we are left disgusted with images.

In its urban incoherence, Naples is the finest example of the fact that the results of absolute disorder are the same as the results of absolute order.

Beside the Étang de Sainte-Périne,[5] the mongols[6] take their Sunday walk. They scare the ducks, which take flight and skid on the frozen surface. Whatever can the ducks be thinking as they suddenly slide out of control on the pond where they dabble the whole year round? And what can be going through the minds of the mongols, beaming and wild-eyed, who look you in the eye without any idea of the image they are presenting, and their monstrous nature? Perhaps the same idea of happiness hovers in both their minds and those of the ducks?

Pompeii.
   The charm of catastrophe is that it has no equivalent in real time. If we revive it in some form of virtual reality, we destroy it. Yet that is what is being planned today: Euro-Pompeii as a live 'spectacular' with a 'reality show' of the eruption of Vesuvius, etc. Pompeii vitrified, vacuum-sealed, Pompeii buried beneath flows of

5. A small lake between La Croix St-Ouen and Pierrefonds in the forêt de Compiègne.
6. It always seems inappropriate to opt for a 'politically correct' usage with Baudrillard. The French term here is 'mongolien'.

tourist lava today serves as a bargaining counter for all future catastrophe simulations. The equivalent of the closed, forbidden cave of Lascaux, which serves as archaeological gold reserve and stock exchange.

They say planetary communications abolish distance. But the impact of catastrophes still remains inversely proportional to distance: 5,000 dead in China are not the equivalent of ten Western lives. In this regard, things are even worse than they once were, since in the past the indifference could be put down to a lack of communications. With that obstacle removed, we can confirm that, beneath the formal solidarity, the discrimination is absolute.

One day, the species will have no other choice but the genetic countdown, that translucent form of suicide which consists in listing all the genes and wresting them from their uselessness. It will find this terminally boring, but it will be too late then for de-escalation. No doubt it is already too late to halt the processes currently in train.

Only something which has a purpose comes to an end, since once that purpose is achieved, all that remains is for it to disappear. The human species has survived only because it had no final purpose. Those who have tried to give it one have generally sent it hurtling to its destruction. And it is perhaps out of some survival instinct that groups and individuals are gradually abandoning any precise purpose, abandoning meaning, reason and the Enlightenment to retain only the untutored, intuitive understanding of an imprecise situation.

Thanks to their contagious solidarity with the low opinion the citizens have of themselves, pity and ridicule are still the politicians' best weapons for gaining votes. This has been of great advantage to Chirac. His appearance on the *Guignols*[7] has served as a kind of expiatory sacrifice. The trick is to draw the sentimental ferociousness of the masses to yourself.

'It isn't the man who drinks the tea, it's the tea which drinks the man'[8]
It isn't you who smoke the pipe, it's the pipe which smokes you
It's the book which reads me
It's the TV which watches you
It's the object which thinks us
It's the lens which focuses on us
It's the effect which causes us
It's language which speaks us
It's time which wastes us
It's money which earns us
It's death which lies in wait for us

7. French TV show, not unlike Britain's 'Spitting Image'.
8. *Ce n'est pas l'homme qui boit le thé, mais le thé qui boit l'homme* is the title of André Maugé's translation of Guido Ceronetti's *Pensieri del Tè*, Adelphi Edizione, Milan 1986.

Virus informatiques (computer viruses)? No: it is information itself which is a virus.

Illness? No: it is health at all costs, the hygienic design of the body – soon to become its genetic design – which is pathological.

Disneyland, Disneyworld? No: these are merely the ephiphenomena of 'real' America, which is entirely Disneyfied.

Corruption, embezzlement? No: this is, rather, the corrective to the crazed, systematic circulation of money. Insider trading? A corrective to the crazed circulation of information. This is all a sham criminality, laundering the fundamental reality of Evil.

Mitterrand's duplicity is not so much the cynical duplicity of the politician as the bourgeois duplicity of the private sphere of personal reserve. His dissimulating isn't that of the Prince, but that of the sentimental moralist in disgrace.

In the end, the Disney Company will no longer even need to buy up companies or invest. Districts, towns and entire populations will ask to be attached to Disney Unlimited, will themselves request entry to the Fourth Dimension.

To understand all, and hence to forgive all, is an unworkable moral law. You can understand the adulteress, and hence forgive her, and hence avoid stringing her up in the town square. But you can also understand the mullah who orders that she be strung up, and even understand the tree she is hanged on, and even the rope. You can understand everything, except that things should be this way.

The most obnoxious thing about the Palestinian terrorists is that they get themselves killed in their attacks. This is cheating. They pledge their deaths as the price to be paid. This is unacceptable. These people don't have the courage to fight fair.

The rain which redoubles in violence before it stops. The water which speeds up as it comes to the waterfall. The athlete who 'ties up' as victory approaches. Hypersensitivity to final conditions.

New urban figure: the man standing on the street corner, mobile phone in hand, or wheeling around like some limp beast, still talking away to no one. A living insult to the passers-by. Only madmen and alcoholics can flout public space in this way, talking to themselves. But they at least are connected up to their inner madness. Whereas mobile-phone-man imposes on everyone – who has no interest in it whatsoever – the virtual presence of the network, which is public enemy number one.

One day the only people left on the streets will be zombies – one group with their mobile phones, the other with their headphones or video headsets. Everyone will be simultaneously elsewhere. They already are. In the past, you could isolate yourself internally. Now you can isolate yourself externally, can retreat into the outer core of your being. Confinement in prison is giving way to the mobile confinement of the network, just as *rigor mortis* has given way to the corpse-like flexibility of switching-man, protean man, Nietzsche's 'chameleon'.

Metronomic regularity of the neighbours' existence, perceived solely from the sounds which, coming through the walls, indicate their presence, their odd habits, their schedules, their daily rituals, their departures. Implacable.

Future cities will merely be subsidiaries of the airports, just as current cities are merely terminals for the motorways which crisscross the land.

The future airport will be 75 miles from Paris. Supposing they build it to the north, and Brussels airport is built at the same distance from that city to the south, they will have only to merge the two airports to take us from the one city to the other. There will no longer be any need to take off. Everything will have merged in the same flight area. A single great air terminal for a unified Europe. You will have only to take the secondary connections for Frankfurt, London, Madrid. In other words, things will be exactly as they were before, but inside the European aeropolis. Or, even better, a world air terminal. The planet turned into one great air terminal, so that journeys take place, in corrected real time, inside the same network. You could even look at the possibility of getting rid of all the planes, since there would no longer be any point to air traffic.

If the film of history stopped dead today, could we say that, from the standpoint of the species, the balance sheet was positive? In the most recent centuries, the human race has increased and multiplied, and has aspired to total mastery of the world and to its transformation. Unfortunately, there is a danger we shall be judged on this very latest period. That is the worst thing that could happen to us.

Proponents of globalization, the Internet and Virtual Reality or nostalgic activists for the Universal and moral values – what does it matter what stand we take on all this! The globe resists globalization; the universe resists the universal.

The last rites was a sacrament borne only very reluctantly, since, if you survived, you had to abstain from all sexual relations. As though death were one of the sexually transmitted diseases.

Sex without a condom now exists only in fiction. Only novels and films preserve the memory of free copulation, with no precautions – old, immoral practices which future generations will doubtless laugh at unrestrainedly. What will they make of these irresponsible images of entwined couples obeying the dictates of pleasure alone? But they will understand the eroticism of chastity belts even less.

When an object is exactly like another, it is not exactly like it, it is a bit more exact.

When we talk about space and the cosmos, it is as though we were talking about the future, whereas the past and origins are always buried in the depths of the Earth (except in *2001, A Space Odyssey*, with its sensational return to origins, deep in the vast reaches of space).

So, the Big Bang is an event which in a sense awaits us in the future of science, and indeed awaits us as an inaccessible horizon. The light of ultra-distant stars is part of a past which has not yet caught up with us, and hence part of our future.

An anamorphosis of time and space occurs here, the distinction between the three dimensions of time ultimately being valid only on our planetary scale. This distinction is fading now in the face of real time.

The USA is parachuting peace into Bosnia in just the same way it as parachuted war into the Gulf. A technological and diplomatic 'ready-made'. As a result, both peace and war seem equally spectral and unreal.

Shame and hatred are interdependent. Two noble and primitive emotions, but when they are combined, they produce the negative passion of repentance.

Thought is nothing but a happy coincidence.

Her objects are permanent fixtures. She doesn't throw any of them away. She cares for them the way she cares for her body. They cannot be allowed to die before she does. The humbler and more wretched they are, the more they have the right to exist. This is all they have left – existence. It is the same with her. And it is not much. Those who do great things do not need to exist. Existence is for the poor – the poor in desire, the poor in pleasure, the poor in spirit. The rich have projects, the poor have only their objects.

So, behind the self-effacement and modesty, there was this resolve, this pride, which showed through only in death. Even when she was young and beautiful, and no doubt desirable, she never knew this. In life, as in death, this silence and discretion leave behind an image of someone at peace with herself, which balances up the image of the father – sorrowful and irresolute.

Unless you have desired it and premeditated it, you cannot really envisage the death of someone close to you. There is no imagining of death. It is absolutely self-evident, and you cannot form an idea of something that is absolutely self-evident.

The gardens of the Château de Compiègne. The frosts, the sadness, the foggy vistas with a few erotic or academic statues of vestals or ephebes shining out, condemned as they are to spend the winter in imperial solitude. A Chloe shrouded in mist, yet with her nubile charm intact, having landed up by chance in this artificially noble landscape, with the ceremonial air of a death mask.

The exhilaration of women among themselves, an exhilaration produced by deliverance from the opposite sex, which now forms the theme of an infinite narrative, but as something distanced. The complicity between men, when they too are among their own kind, is of this same order, no doubt – a complicity that is different from homosexuality, stemming from deliverance from the presence of women. Intellectuals among themselves represent a singular case: their collusive joy comes from being rid of both sexes at once.

Suddenly, she had a wild desire to take the little black cat in her arms. In other words, a desire for someone to take her in their arms. A sudden desire to be cradled and to become once again an adorable little thing who would never grow up – and certainly not an ambassador's wife.

The unexpectedness of love was not so great as her surprise at escaping for once, as though in a dream, from her familiar world, and feeling a stranger to herself. For the first time in her life, no one knew what she was doing or where she was (I alone knew, but I wasn't part of her life).

The latest psychological and therapeutic wheeze: for a speeding offence, as an alternative to a heavy fine, you'll be able to choose viewing a road-safety film and having a session with a psychologist. The last I heard, they had gone one better. The offender is to be brought face to face with a survivor of a serious road accident.

Jesuitical apotheosis of moral re-education, of redemption by the contrition and indulgences which keep us out of Hell, only to hurl us into the torments of purgation.

St Petersburg.

All along the walls of the Peter and Paul Fortress, in the first days of spring the sunbathers of perestroika offer themselves up naked – or almost naked – to the sun's exterminating rays. They seem to hang from the red ochre wall, as though thrown against it by some kind of centrifugal force. Like the irradiated silhouettes of Hiroshima, or the skeletons of the Convento dei Cappuccini at Palermo. Or like the Mur des Fusillés or the Wailing Wall, or like the Platonic shadows on the walls of the cave, or those bodies in Signorelli's fresco at Orvieto only half emerging from the earth, covered with a colourless, barely resuscitated flesh – this is what the pale bodies of St Petersburg look like, hardly out of winter limbo yet, freshly dug up and propped there motionless, their eyes closed, men and women all mingled together, like torture victims.

A strange ritual, this show of flesh in the middle of the city, this solar prostitution, which resembles nothing so much as an execution. On the very site where thousands of political prisoners were tortured to death by the Tsars.

On one side, the immense pollution, the immense metropolitan hum of Bogotá rising towards the monastery, towards the Way of the Cross with its copper faces. On the other side of the ridge, the total silence of the equatorial forest.

Dozens of public letter-writers are set up in the streets with their 1950s typewriters, surrounded by illiterates who have never known writing. Just beside them the modern executives scuttle by. Already they, equipped as they are with their mobile phones, no longer know what it is to write.

Seen from a walkway at some commemorative event at the Cité de la Villette, the entire scientific and cultural community, thronging around the buffets, seems to be afflicted with baldness, like a community of moulting apes or anthropoids – the bald heads alternating with the women's bare shoulders.

We know that society life in general attests to desperate disappointment at the real conditions of existence.

The fire at the Crédit Lyonnais, miraculously destroying all the files while sparing the monumental staircase (the heritage) and the phynance coffers (the capital).[9] A good move: such misfortune cannot but arouse public compassion, and so wipe away the traces of the scam. This will be some consolation to the taxpayers when they have to stump up the 150 billion francs to pay off the debts.

Such an event is never accidental. If it were, it would be even too good to be true.

Unlike intellectuals, who are obsessed with meaning, the masses long since sensed that the only empire – the only power – is that of signs.

We have a dangerous tendency to set less store by *appearances* than by *being*, less store by phenomena than by their causes, less store by the immobility of things than by their motives.

If there is an ineradicable memory of cells, the way there is a memory of water, then will my cells in another life retain a trace of the soft grass of the île Ste. Lucie[10] on that June afternoon? And will the molecules of the grass have also retained the electromagnetic trace of my epidermis? That fusion is already made anyway in the simple mental continuity of sensations. It is marvellous that every being in nature

9. The fire at the headquarters of the troubled Crédit Lyonnais took place on 5 May 1996. The spelling 'phynance' is Alfred Jarry's.
10. An island in the Étang de Bages et de Sigean, south of Narbonne.

should remember all the others. The idea that, in the world of networks and artificial memories, everyone should remember everything – and everything remember you – is monstrous.

The only real recreation: the stunned contemplation of elementary phenomena – the myriads of sand fleas gambolling around on the edge of the incoming tide, the water advancing up the beach by fractions of an inch, the Lilliputian forms of a meaningless repetition. The best thing there is for inducing mental stupefaction. In the evenings, the luminescent bellies of the nocturnal insects – alive and dead – lighten the darkness of the *bergerie*.

Strange sea. While there has been not a breath of wind for several days, and the sea seems perfectly flat out in the bay, long, stormy waves break upon the beach, as though whipped up by some undersea breeze.

The north wind puts an end to all this, restoring wind and sky to their normal tumultuous state. Amid these atmospheric stirrings, the sky changes so quickly that the sun seems to be charging across the clouds, the way it passes across the body of Osiris in Egyptian wall paintings.

Once the video eye takes root everywhere, daily life is no longer a subject for novels. Once the sociological eye and ideology settle themselves into all passions, they are no longer a subject for fict on. Once aesthetics infiltrates the everyday world, art is no longer a source of illusion. Once facts come under the aegis of information, they are no longer objects of knowledge. Insider trading:

everyone knows too much. Knowledge devastates phenomena, the idea devastates reality.

Information is not knowledge, it is making-known, and this has its counterpart in making-out-that-one-knows – in pretend knowledge. Propaganda, ideology and advertising are not belief, but making-believe, which has its response in making-out-that-one-believes – in pretend belief. Television is not seeing, it is making-see, the corresponding reaction being to make out that one sees – pretend seeing. We are prisoners of facticity: of making-see, making-believe, making-out, etc. We are no longer the direct agents of our acts and thoughts. We are merely heteromobile vehicles, who have set their vital functions to automatic pilot and become indifferent to themselves. Simulating finality in a transfinal process.

   Truth is born of disillusion.
   The real is born of lack of imagination.

The imagining of thought is more precious than thought itself.

We are all the living victims of unconscious flows, which simply come together in us. The dead part pulls the living along, like those worms where one part of the body wriggles forward and drags all the rest along.

The great liturgical ceremony of the Chiapas. All the Western *nomenklatura* there to commune together in a distant echo of Aztec sacrifices and the International

Brigades. But the echo, too, of another event some four centuries ago, when a little further down the Brazilian coast, newly Christianized Indians were gathered on the beach for a conversion Mass, in the presence of Jesuit dignitaries and bishops who had travelled from Rome. They became seized, towards the end of the ceremony, with a convivial enthusiasm, rushed the missionaries and devoured them. What if the Lacandones were also suddenly gripped with an amorous frenzy for these higher brethren, come to immolate themselves on the altar of revolt? What if they took a sudden notion to perform a blood sacrifice? Just deserts – the intellectuals long having drawn their substance from the cannibalization of lesser brothers.

The ideological exploitation of the victims of poverty is ultimately not so very different from the trade in blood and organs: it's all part of the Western world's import–export business. It would be logical, then, for this victimal nostalgia to end in a real sacrifice, for the auto-da-fé to end in a hetero-da-fé and for anthropology to end where it began – in anthropophagy.

Atlanta: the same spectacle as when the Roman gladiators came in from the ends of the Empire to fight to the death for the entertainment of the Roman populace. In this case, it is the world's black, brown and mixed-race peoples competing on all the planet's TV screens. Times have changed. And so have the stakes. In Rome, the losers were put to death. Among the Aztecs, it was the winners who were executed, competing for that supreme honour. Today, the athletes are happy just to visualize the winner's rostrum.

All that remains now is to make sex an Olympic discipline: the Sex Olympics. With, as in Atlanta, Parallel Games for the sexually disabled.

Stuck for hours on the motorway with his family, a tourist declares: 'Well, you know, we're on holiday. Here or the beach, what does it matter?' The need to be nowhere – this is what drives the hordes out on to the roads. And nowhere means anywhere but home. It's the same with work and leisure: drudgery in the one place, drudgery in the other. The moment of freedom comes in moving from one drudgery to another. And if you go away, it isn't to wipe out the effects of the eight daily hours of forced labour, but to compensate for not being forced to work twenty-four hours a day, as the higher executives do – people who have no need of holidays.

Laughable scenes of stock farmers who have travelled up from their provincial backwaters to ascend the steps of the Élysée Palace, where they will be spontaneously hoodwinked by a President who resembles nothing so much as a cattle trader.

The idea of power must have fallen very low for us to demand certificates of health or morality from our leaders – a medical warrant of fitness for the exercise of power. As though the cancer of the President (Mitterrand) could contaminate the nation. As though he were no longer representative of the State, but of the state of the nation's health. In days gone by, men in power were entitled to be hypocritical, murderous, ambitious and corrupt in exchange for their symbolic sacrifice (the weight of responsibility, the risk of death). Today, they meet with the opposite fate: they aren't even entitled to be ill any more. They have to prove their fitness, their virtue. This is an idiotic demand, and it sums up our democracy. You can understand why Mitterrand refused to give in to this humiliating 'openness'. And you understand his hypocrisy too: why not throw such imbeciles off his trail?

So long as the universe was thought to be 5,000 years old, as it says in the Bible, we knew where we were. Since we went beyond these bounds, the age of the universe has been constantly going up and down, as the findings of science have ordained. Once 'released' from superstition, the date of the origin became uncertain. And it will be increasingly so. The Bible's 5,000 years had an infinite depth to it (it was the 'mists of time'), an impenetrable profundity. By contrast, our dating can only perpetually outstrip itself in a kind of world record attempt (in a 'very short time' we have gone from three to eight million years for the human race). The time horizon recedes as the definition of time itself disappears into the mists of the origins of species.

Without images, nothing takes place. Below 10 per cent audience figures, no event is worthy of credence. Conversely, when you speak to an audience of more than ten people, there can be no question of challenging reality – you meet with immediate rejection. Which proves that this much-vaunted reality is both magical and statistical in nature.

Mallarmé: 'Reality is an artifice, good only for finding the average intellect a foothold among the mirages of a fact. But in that very pursuit, it depends on some universal agreement' (*Gossips*).

It would be interesting to verify the existence of reality with surveys, as has just been done for the existence of God: 'Do you believe in reality?' The results would be posted everywhere, providing a constant display of the rate of global reality as measured by public opinion (the way they post up the national debt figure on billboards in New York).

True poverty lies in the economic calculation of life. It is the same with the calculation of thought. The production of multiple 'objective' truths is a zero-sum accumulation (we shall always still be as far away from exhaustively accounting for the world). Similarly, the unchecked accumulation of ideas and culture is the astronomical sign of our intellectual poverty.

You can be very intelligent and very stupid, very lively and very lethargic at the same time. It is this isomorphism of incoherent traits, this 'idiosyncrasy', which makes it almost impossible to correct a character.

Better: character depends on this basic contrariness – the indecipherable constellation of two contradictory qualities forming a single characteristic, in the same way as two contradictory meanings are merged in a single witticism.

In this sense, character is destiny. Those whose character structure is not internally contradictory and who live out their psychological being directly, without irony, are insignificant beings, the products at best of a 'personal equation' and a basic formula. Destiny lies in the *détournement* of this basic psychological formula. And the ideal relationship is one in which both parties collude in the internally contradictory play of their natural characters.

The Siamese twin sisters: neither the one nor the other; neither differentiated nor undifferentiated. What if one of them goes mad? What if they fall out hopelessly? And what happens when one is sleeping and the other isn't? And what does one do while the other is dreaming? Can they even fall in love with each other?

Deep down, we are all Siamese twins: in each of us one part sleeps and the other is awake; one part decides and the other resigns itself to its fate; one part desires and the other denies itself, etc.

Things which are still running on out of sheer inertia.

The Russian cosmonaut on his orbit after the end of the USSR.

Ballard's astronauts, who died long ago and became perpetual satellites.

Alfred Jarry's Siberian five-man bicycle, with its cycling corpses which go on pedalling.[11]

The TWA Boeing, cut in two by a missile, but with the back half continuing on its course with all its passengers.

St Denis, the bishop of Paris, striding on with his severed head in his hands.[12]

The high-wire artist carrying on along a nonexistent wire.

The political, economic and cultural institutions which persist on their path into the void, like headless chickens.

11. In the 'Ten-Thousand-Mile Race', which is recounted by Alfred Jarry in *The Supermale* (Exact Change, Cambridge 1999), pp. 49–71.

12. St Denis and two companions were tortured and executed around AD 275. Legend has it that the bishop's decapitated corpse rose and carried his severed head for some distance.

Gathering the fragments of the TWA Boeing one by one from the bottom of the sea and storing them away in vacuum packs: an Identikit picture of the catastrophe which we'll never get to the bottom of. Perhaps one day all this debris will be built into a Museum of the Unknown Accident. Simultaneously, they are raising the cabin of the *Titanic* from the depths of the ocean. Ancient disasters and recent catastrophes – everything is resurfacing as part of the obsessive desire to refloat time itself. Reviving the fatal moment – this is what we dream of. It is that moment which has sunk and become a piece of wreckage; it is time which has been destroyed in mid-flight.

As with sleep and dreaming, there could be said to be a paradoxical time and a deep time.[13] A time when you dream of time, and a time without dreams. To each his own way of winding along the time snake.

A film by Charles Najman, *Can Memory Be Dissolved in Evian Water?* How can the survivors of the extermination camps agree to come here for treatment paid for by the heirs to the final solution? How can they accept this posthumous charity and undergo the sinister therapeutic comedy of spa cures: showers, flotation tanks, carbon dioxide baths – an entire remake, to crown it all, of the agony of the

13. 'Paradoxical sleep' is another term for what is more commonly known in English as rapid eye movement or REM sleep.

concentration camps? Why do they do it? They do it because they have never got over it. Because those who survived have never forgiven themselves, and are forever amazed still to be here – just alive enough to relive their primal scene each year.

The genius of the human species is to have added remorse to pleasure, with a view to achieving heightened pleasure. To have increased wealth with the spectacle of poverty, misery with commiseration, sentiment with *Ressentiment.*

Towards the end of adolescence, you think most people and things (except the most beautiful) have no right to exist. At a more advanced age, you get into an opposite confusion: everything has a right to exist – which makes the world equally unbearable.

Some women show off their bodies and overaccentuate this with adornment. Others unveil their bodies, while retaining the mystery. Yet others make their bodies disappear purely and simply beneath veils which discourage the imagination.

He is perfectly qualified to talk about destiny by virtue of the fact that no existence is as remarkable as his for its absence of destiny.
     You have to be alive to talk about death.

Theatre of Cruelty in New York. What can you say about Artaud except that not everyone has the good fortune to be mad. What can you say of Warhol except that not everyone has the good fortune to be a machine. That's our hard luck. Here we are. We are what we are.

The veil of insomnia, like the film of white on eggs-over-easy or the veiled eyelids of the octopus.

In the eyes of each girl, the smile of the day.
In the eyes of the teachers, the smile of the month.
In the eyes of the 'Halloween' children, the rictus of the year.

Only those poisoned by bad conscience get stressed out. The businessman, moving in a stressed, 'hyper' atmosphere, tuning in and out at will, regenerates automatically and has no build-up of toxins. He lives under hypnosis, and so has no need of sleep. He is simultaneously awake and asleep, like horses and fish.

All the newspapers are full of a limited theory of current events, in which each one is taken on its own. But if you take them all together, you see a strange convergence. The attack on Bordeaux Town Hall, the fire at Crédit Lyonnais and the bomb at Port-Royal: coincidences that are too good to be true.[14] No need for a

14. These events took place on 6 October 1996, 5 May 1996 and 25 July 1996 respectively. The Port-Royal referred to is the metro station of that name, where seven people were killed by a terrorist device. The bomb at the Palais Rohan in Bordeaux did serious material damage, but caused no deaths.

strategy: the conspiracy operates automatically. The fire, the 'accident', the 'attack' provide automatic get-outs from some dubious situations. They are precisely not accidents. But the truth merely complicates things. Always coming retrospectively, it is itself almost a part of the conspiracy.

Paedophilia, unemployment, mad-cow disease: the three events of the year – non-events, anti-events; even unemployment, which is only ever the irresistible decline of the social dimension in slow motion. The only significant relationship between the three is that they do not originate in the political sphere, and do not return there.

There are precedents for mad-cow disease: Io, the heifer beloved of Zeus and bitten by a fly; and, above all, Danaë, the mad exile who gave birth to the Danaïdes, who filled their bottomless barrel not with water but with blood.

All the ills of the falsely intellectualized political class have in their turn infected an intellectual class which has become politicized by stealth: cynicism, fundamental-ism, opportunism, blackmail and corruption.

Proposal for a new law: all the speculators whose ill-gotten gains exceed the earn-ings of an average worker over the course of his or her working life will be sentenced to death.

To claim to speak of death, or the world's woes,[15] or anything else 'objectively' is an illusion, for language is always more real than what it speaks about.

The key thing is to clear the mental space. What happens after that, what emerges in this void, is no longer your responsibility. It is a question put to the world, not a question put to philosophy.

What is the point of writing? Since the 'accursed share' became a magic potion, the most radical analysis serves merely as a vaccine and a laxative. By reactivating criticism, you render the objective fury of the facts bloodless.

There is no call to reinvent critical, philosophical judgement. You can only set one vision against another, one radicality against another.

> Moralistic: if you don't believe in reality, you're an impostor.
> Fanatical: if you don't believe in reality, you're not fit to exist.
> Democratic: if you don't believe in truth, don't turn others against it.

In *Leaving Las Vegas*, you see a young blonde woman calmly taking a pee and wiping herself while she carries on talking, indifferent to what she is saying and

---

15. The French phrase here is 'les misères du monde', which is the title of a work by Pierre Bourdieu, translated into English as *The Weight of the World* (Polity, Cambridge 1999).

doing. The scene is perfectly pointless. But it signifies conspicuously that nothing must escape the fade-in/fade-out of reality and fiction, that nothing escapes the show-all, see-all culture. That is what transparency is: forcing the whole of the real into the orbit of representation. The obscene is what is uselessly visible – needlessly, with no desire involved and no effect achieved. Which usurps the – so rare and precious – space of appearances.

After the natural selection of species, the natural selection of artificial creatures. Every day thousands of sites die on the Internet. What began in the world of living beings is carrying on in the world of digital, genetic, cybernetic artefacts, doomed to disappear in droves to leave room for just a few of their kind, or for their distant descendants in the digital chain. And this is just the beginning of this ruthless selection process. In the chain of the Virtual, we are more or less at the stage represented in the order of life by bacteria.

She is an expert diver in the clear waters of the tropical seas. I practise that sport in the mental depths and in deep metaphorical waters – in the sea-green universe of the concept. There, too, you need a mask and you're never certain you'll resurface. You have to come back gradually, by stages, to the amphibian space of reality. You have each time to relive the migration of aquatic species to *terra firma*.

She is not afraid to confront her phantasms – both the marine and the underwater ones. Her primal scene is one she immerses herself in totally. *Son beau corps a roulé sous la vague marine.*[16] Now, if women *fulfil* their dreams (amorous, nuptial, conjugal or fusional), what can they still dream of? And how can we dream of them when they 'fulfil' themselves? How can we dream of wildness when we are really up close to wild creatures?

'Male utopias are over, long live female utopias!' Now, women have never had any utopias of their own – they *are* utopia! And if they fulfil themselves as women, then that is fulfilled, achieved utopia. But achieved utopia is a dangerous, paradoxical situation.

Have you noticed how 'liberated women' have retained the essential characteristic of 'alienated' ones, which consists in systematically arriving late?

You know that woman. She has made the reputation of a whole city. She is made of linen and hemp; and her plumage is natural. Delicate but solidly built, she is specially designed to preserve the taste and aroma of your preferred phantasms.

Brazilians, male and female, when they get excited about what they are saying, do

16. This is a line from André Chénier's poem 'La Jeune Tarentine':

> Elle est au sein des flots la jeune Tarentine!
> Son beau corps a roulé sous la vague marine.

not raise their voices. They introduce a tremor into them – high-pitched, contralto, or a modulated growl.

Menopausal aphrodites rising moist from the sea into the encroaching evening, their breasts, in gentle confinement, swinging their critical mass into the sea breeze, while their fleshy rears are offered up to the parabolic mirror of concupiscence.

Brazilians (of both sexes) have a way of being more naked than us, because they are naked from the inside. We merely take our clothes off.

In the stews and stockpots of Bahian cooking, you always think you can see decoction of missionary, so much is Brazilian affection a thing of eating and cannibalism, flattering and caressing you as it does, as through you were its prey. You always think you can see in their eyes: 'How delicious he was, my little Frenchman!'

Woman came out of the male imagination. In every sense: she was a product of that imagination, and she has escaped from its grasp (never to return?). Women have become real, whereas they were once conspicuous by their absence.

Just as shadows are produced by the sun being intercepted by a physical body, so Doubles are produced by the Subject intercepting the sun of otherness. We have, alas, become transparent, and we have lost our shadows. We have become translucent, and we have lost our doubles. Or is it the light source of otherness which has disappeared?

Even if it has slipped into the dead man's place to feed on you, that living monster, the audience, is still one of the living dead. In the TV studio, on the other hand, you are under the eye of a virtual monster, a line of gazes, licking you with its tactile eye, as in a peepshow. A lecture audience you can keep warm in the dark, in a palpable obscurity. The TV audience puts you into the sensory neutrality of a flotation tank. If, for the ordinary public, which feeds on words, you are still a living object of desire, for the remote visual sensors you are a dead one. That is why the finest revenge is to watch a programme you have refused to take part in.

There is no other world. We are in it. This is the other world. So there will be no end to this one. And there will be no other.

We are no longer in a culture of Good and Evil, but in the culture of the Better, whose mirror-equivalent is the Worse. So everything is getting simultaneously better and better, and worse and worse.

They say that old watches begin systematically to gain. Are they impatient for the end to come?

The tide of funds sweeping into culture, social welfare and the Third World clearly has no other purpose than to mop up the excess of money that is poisoning the Western economies. And those who believe they are doing something for the have-nots with all these programmes – most of which go straight down the drain – are merely taking on this vital function of consumption which the deprived are, in the main, forced to assume, thus becoming its victims. For the same exploited peoples from whom in the past we extracted a surplus now serve ('into the bargain') to digest and absorb that surplus. Entire populations are doomed to the contradictory, twofold labour of being despoiled for profit and mobilized like digestive enzymes, like bacteria in septic tanks.

Where art is concerned, the most interesting thing would be to insinuate oneself into the spongiform encephalon of the modern spectator. For that is where the mystery lies today: in the brain of the recipient, the nerve centre of this servile attitude to current 'works of art'. What is the secret of it? The spectators take the mortifications which the 'creative artists' inflict on objects and their own bodies and, in a mirroring collusion, inflict them on themselves and their own mental faculties. This is what I have called the 'art conspiracy'. Hence, in aesthetic matters, the substantial raising of the threshold of tolerance of the worst.

Reviving the idea of the Institute for Astral Surgery, where you can (for quite a high price) change your star sign, like your face, if you are not happy with it. But how are we to go about this? First by putting the patients into the same planetary conjunction as pertained at their birth, then displacing an orbit or a trajectory slightly. Or, alternatively, by taking the desired sign from another person (at their death) and transplanting it, as is done with any other organ. Since there is some risk of rejection with this operation, coefficients of astrological immunity will have to be studied. A star-sign bank may have to be created.

This project can be combined with the plans for a Suicide Motel, in which you can have yourself 'suicided,' if you don't have the courage to perform the act yourself. If the astral surgery is not successful, the client will always be free to call on the services of the Suicide Motel (at no extra charge).

The signs by which a woman seduces you are principally the signs by which she enjoins you to seduce her. Hence the dread of the seducer, who cannot but respond. That obligation is enough to render a woman irresistible. The woman, for her part, cannot but respond to the honour one does her in wishing to seduce her. There is no question in all this of desire and concupiscence. Seduction is a homage. No good is to be expected of a man who does not make it a point of honour. Nor of a woman who does not stake her honour on being seduced.

Sunday Mass at Leucate.[17] Theme of the peroration: Jesus and his disciples beside the Sea of Galilee. How is it that Jesus is overwhelmed by tiredness, when a word from him is enough to calm the raging waves? Well, my brothers, it is because Christ is of a twofold nature (human and divine) in a single person, whereas God is three persons (Father, Son and Holy Spirit) in a single nature.

After this extraordinary theological exordium, which the congregation do not remotely understand, the priest moves on very quickly to other matters closer to

17. Leucate is a seaside town between Perpignan and Narbonne.

their lives: the Vatican's accounts, the Church's finances and the Pope's visit. With the Pope, things are simpler: one person, one nature.

If life has a meaning, any form of incompletion becomes a taint, a crime, a failing. An unbearable tension sets in, which only death can end. So every effort to give life meaning is an enterprise of demoralization.

Today, however, it is paradoxically because life no longer has any meaning that we have to do the most we can with it. It is because God is dead that we have to glorify His name.

Ants, too, must know that God is dead, since they engage in such frantic activity. Is it to avoid internal revolts and boredom that they have developed such a relentless programme (not too different, perhaps, from the human race)? Have they developed a cult of the absurd or some crazed ritual for turning life and its meaning to their own perverse ends? Have they invented a perfect model of cloning, the only way of guaranteeing the eternity of a species and solving the problem of individual existence? A wonderful hypothesis, but how can we know? Let them speak, these ants, let them confess! What is their message? Yet they just go on walking enormous distances to bring back things that are actually plentiful around the anthill (in this, too, they are not so different from the human race).

The monument to communication in the Bay of Osaka. Several hundred tons of granite transplanted from the Bay of Roscoff to the sacred island of Awaji, which, according to ancient myth, was the first island created by the gods. On 17 January

1995, the first granite block was taken to the site. Five days later, the Kobe earthquake occurred, with its epicentre two kilometres away. Clearly, the gods do not smile on Universal Communications. Are they going to give up the project? Not at all. They're going to build a 'meditation hall' beneath the building in honour of the 6,000 victims of the earthquake. Above this the Museum/Monument will rise up – a portal to cyberspace where all the nations of the globe will be able to bask in virtual reality.

An even more terrible vengeance of the gods is to be feared.

And what if the world itself had been silent at first, as the cinema was, and still like photographs, before moving on to the 'talking' stage, then a stereoscopic, 3-D phase and in the end becoming virtual, like the reality of the same name? Becoming digital – that is to say, passing into the Fourth Dimension, where everything has become not silent, but aphasic; not aphonic, but stereophonic; fractal, but without relief and depth; visual, but without image. Fundamentally, the world might be said to have the same destiny as the cinema, which might be seen as its abbreviated, accelerated form – like a whole life flashing before you when you faint.

On waking, the pattern of the dream fades, but its aura, ambience, timbre and tonality remain, though there is no image. It's the same with a piece of music. You have it in your mind, you can hear it mentally, but you can't summon it up as form. Or with a face, whose features and smile you can feel in a tactile way, but with no recall of what it looks like. Where on earth does this force of the dream register itself, this reminiscence without image?

The one fantastic moment is that moment of first contact, when things have not yet noticed we are there, when they have not yet fallen in with the order of analysis. It is the same with language: when it has not yet had time to signify. Or with deserts: when their silence is still intact and our absence has not had time to dissipate. . . . But that instant is ephemeral; it is gone in a trice. You would have to not be there to see it. Perhaps only ghosts experience that exceptional pleasure.

Is it an imposture to make improbable statements without appearing to do so, to stun people into silence with paradoxes and catch imaginations unawares? Then long live the rightful use of imposture!

Those speeches, lectures and dinners where the absurdity of the situation releases an inner delight; in which boredom transmutes into a convulsive, silent joy, into a mirth painfully contained beneath the mask demanded by protocol.

To protect sheep from dingoes, the Australians are building a fence which runs right across the continent. Separating prey from their predators represents a violence even worse than the natural violence of species.

You could imagine burying the dead with their mobiles, so that we can contact them in the hereafter. This fictional scenario became a tragic reality when, on the charred bodies left by the fire in the Gothenburg discotheque, the mobile phones continued to ring.

All forms of information leave us with a sense of mystification. And rightly so: where 'truth' is concerned, everything is hidden from us. But there is, ultimately, nothing to hide – no secret, no plot and no truth. And this is hidden from us too, which is a more subtle mystification.

In the classical imagination, Evil was still a mythical power. There was still a Mephisto or a Frankenstein to embody the principle of Evil. Our evil is faceless and without imagination. We no longer need the Devil to steal our shadows. There are no powers doing battle above our heads, fighting over our souls. No longer any need for the lubricious agency of capital to extort our labour-power from us. We no longer have any shadows, any souls, and we are stakeholders in our own lives.

Where accidents happen in succession, there is a kind of instinctive relationship between them. Having once smelled blood, they come running with a passion, impatient to occur in their turn, drawn in by the magnetic field. You become a kind of accident attraction zone. New mothers, for example, are particularly fecund and fertile. We underestimate this capacity which events – particularly unfortunate events – have of reproducing themselves not sexually but by contiguity, by 'kairogenesis'.

When we look at the holocaust perpetrated on primitive societies by successive waves of colonization, we forget that Western civilization performed the crime on itself first, that it carried out the same massacre in the name of a higher order. All 'modern' nations emerged out of the same primal crime, the same colonization of countless 'primitive' languages and cultures, the same ethnic cleansing. Why not, then, also make the others pay the price of their sacrifice – those cultures being, into the bargain, a living source of remorse? Once dead, they serve to fuel nostalgia. But, if it seems that nothing is necessarily going to stop this mechanism of extermination, one question remains: what impulse, deep down in the species, lies at the origin of this ruthless murder, this ruthless suicide?

If you believe in God, He exists as an object of belief, but not then as a transcendent agency. A God who demands that you believe in Him is no longer worthy to command belief.

It is the same with reality. If you believe in reality, it exists as an object of belief, but not then as 'objective' reality. A reality which demands that you believe in it is no longer worthy of this world.

Reality exists, therefore (perhaps), but I do not believe in it. This is the agnostic view: we have no proof of the existence of God, any more than of reality. That is the situation, and there is no point adding in superstition.

The social order teaches you to keep quiet, it does not teach you silence.

In the past, bad literature was made with high-flown sentiment; today, it is made with the unconscious.

Excess of information kills information; excess of meaning kills meaning, etc. But it seems that too much stupidity does not kill stupidity. Stupidity may be said, then, to be the only exponential phenomenon – one which even escapes the laws of physics. This is a miracle to rival perpetual motion.

Night flight to São Paulo. Twelve recumbent figures lying in the shade – like Hopper's figures lying in the sun in their deckchairs in 'High Noon' – being propelled across the Atlantic in their luxury sarcophagus. As you move from economy through to business and then first class, the bodies move closer to the horizontal position of the dead, thanks to the progressive angling of the seats.

Buenos Aires at six in the morning. At this hour the Avenida de Mayo is the most beautiful in the world, deserted as a landing strip. The lights change from red to green with the same regularity – the only trace of artificial light in the world of early morning. On the road out to the airport, the fields are shrouded in mist, with just the treetops and the advertising hoardings peering out in the horizontal sunlight. Everything is so beautiful like this; the day should end here and now.

As jet lag, that delicious hypnagogic state, fades, impatience returns – irritation at the world, the vexation and futility of the real world. It all resurfaces in concentric waves.

No analysis of the vibrations of light will ever explain the sensory imagining of colours. No digital optics will ever explain red in its literalness, in its absolute difference from blue or green, any more than any logic will ever explain the relation of the sign to the thing, of red to the term 'red', which is just as indefinable as red.

The photographer dreams of a hyperborean light, of a rarefied atmosphere in which things take on the exactness they might have in the void. It is also a phantasm of the mind to see an idea, a word or an entire sentence stand out with absolute clarity, with only the flickering which comes from distance – just like the world, which is there too in its entirety, but in a veiled dimension, with just a few fragments emerging from it, touched by actual grace.

A whirl of idiotic events amasses around distraught souls, just as flesh and fat amass around a scar.

Being protected from any serious confrontation with Harm [*le Mal*], the body amuses itself today by falling ill. The new (psychosomatic, autoimmune) illnesses are the original new-found entertainment of a de-cathected body, which no longer knows what to do with itself, other than play with its antibodies. Just as the new technologies are the new-found distractions of a broken-down brain, which no longer knows what to do with itself other than toy with its artificial double.

The same problems that confronted thirteenth-century theologians about the Last Judgement ('shall we be resuscitated in an ideal form or in our physical integrity?') are being faced now, as human beings are projected into an artificial immortality: should the human being be cloned in its physical integrity (as he or she is) or on the basis of some ideal formula?

No faith whatsoever is worthy of another world. No life whatsoever is worthy of a second existence. Yet some situations, some unassuaged passions, seem to demand a continuation and an end in another life.

We claim to be able to do everything ouselves. But the wisest thing is to put one's trust in some other power. So the peasant tills the soil, the gambler throws the dice, the primitive performs the ritual – it is for Nature, Luck, the Gods to do the rest. They are not forced to respond, but you have to give them the chance.

On the walls of the city a picture of a handsome adolescent, happy to be alive. How thoughtless of him! He is unaware that 'in France 30,000 people are HIV-positive without realizing it'. No question of his escaping the jurisdiction of death. If he is not infected with the AIDS virus, at least he will be infected with the virus of advertising and fear.

The latest news is that the life insurance companies are no longer immune from bankruptcy. So we are going to have to take out insurance on our life insurance. Insurance has become as fragile as life.

Information is the paradoxical dream of the community – the hypnotic state in which it might be said to regenerate, along with its collective identity, which is supposed to be the function of dreams in individual life. Or information occupies the place of deep sleep, with real life as the corresponding state of paradoxical wakefulness.

'You have to choose between reality and illusion. There is no middle way. Either everything is real or everything is illusion' (Cioran). In other words, everything is as it is, and that is all there is to it. Or nothing is ever what it is, nor ever has been; everything is altered from the beginning.

To put the choice this way means that the simulacrum no longer exists. Since it operates between illusion and reality, then if we have to choose between the two, the concept of the simulacrum vanishes. It disappears the way the soul and its concept disappeared as an imaginary solution to the relationship between man and God.

In fact, Cioran's dilemma does not apply. Choosing between illusion and reality is impossible. And it is precisely the play of the simulacrum which allows us not to choose. It is not, then, an imaginary solution, and its reign is universal.

We no more believe in star signs or in what the media tell us than primitives believed in their magic or the Greeks in their gods. Only the professionals of belief believe others believe these things. The only superstition is that of scholars and experts.

You have to be very careful with stupidity. Condemning stupidity is an immediately reversible act – by a mirror- or boomerang-effect. It is impossible to point out stupidity without it pointing back at you. Impossible to point up stupidity without showing up intelligence as arrogant.

In the vicinity of intelligence, stupidity becomes more stupid. Around stupidity, intelligence becomes more subtle. The nearer they come to each other, the more they exacerbate each other (often in one and the same person). So much so that they end up merging, wearied and intoxicated by their opposites. Ecstasy of stupidity in the presence of intelligence, ecstasy of intelligence in the presence of stupidity.

Stupid people are those who have no idea of evil (though they may do evil). Intelligent people are those who know evil (but they do not do it). It is not enough merely to be intelligent, then, to be wicked, but it is not sufficient to be stupid either.

The only truly wicked people are those who both know and do evil.

Might not paedophilia be said to be the final stage of the fetishistic promotion of the child – following directly from the child's elevation into the firmament of human rights and the simultaneous relegation of childhood to the purgatory of useless functions? The child recognized as a fully fledged human being naturally becomes also a fully fledged sex object. It was the same with women: their 'liberation' was accompanied by an unlimited sexual availability. And the workers: their 'liberation' has cost them an unlimited industrial servitude. As soon as you are recognized legally, you are marked out as a potential victim.

But childhood knows how to take its revenge. From now on, every adult also becomes a potential paedophile. And children will surely not fail to exploit this victim situation, just as women have done with sexual harassment. As soon as they realize the immense power their rights confer on them, it will be adults and parents who will need protecting from children.

There is a whole collector's market out there for cuddly toys with glass eyes. They change hands at fantastic prices. But fans are interested only if they are virginal – if no child has slept with them or caressed them.

Time as transcendental datum, quite simply as a gift of Heaven. How can we give thanks for Time? How can we pay our debt to it other than by giving it a part in our pleasures and projects, and by repeated engagement in useless activities? But today, even this dimension is getting away from us. Orphans of the past wandering about the 'Ruins of the Future' (Stourdzé), we have now, literally, only dead time – the memory of the time when there was time.

There are any number of desiring subjects, but objects of desire are becoming rarer and rarer. The object in us is ageing more quickly than the subject, and we are ceasing to be objects of desire long before we stop being subjects of desire. Now, isn't it better to be endlessly desired than to desire in vain?

Disappearance is not death, and sadness at a disappearance is not the sadness of mourning. So *saudade* expresses not mourning for what is dead, but nostalgia for what has disappeared, with (as in the case of Sebastian and the Fifth Empire) the glimmer of a hope of resurrection.[18] And what the mothers of the Plaza de Mayo

18. *Saudade*, that peculiarly Portuguese artistic expression of nostalgia, often draws on the mythology of 'Sebastianism', with its belief that the slumbering King Sebastian will one day return to found the 'Quinto Império' or Fifth Empire.

in Buenos Aires were calling for, knowing they would never see their sons again, was a proof of their death, as a release from the anguish of their disappearance.

To see without being seen is a banal phantasm – this is the fate of the voyeur. Being seen without seeing is a more original move – this is the fate of the idol. Capturing the other's gaze without returning it. Many women know how to do this – passing by with indifference, seen from all sides, but seeing nothing, not knowing they are being seen. Some want to love without being loved – that is like seeing without being seen. Others want to be loved without loving in return – that is like being seen without seeing.

The perfect criminal is the one who lays claim to the crime he has not committed. Who conceals his innocence behind the mask of crime. *He* is much harder to unmask.

There is no poverty and no wealth. There is merely an impoverished definition of wealth – in terms of economics and calculation. Unfortunately, the entire world's poor have signed up to this definition, which makes them poor to the second degree.

In a world of spectral identity, anything will do to restore a sense of incarnation – body-piercing and branding, brutishness and bestiality, stress and pressure, stigmata and excrement. Flow of blood, flow of meaning. Alas, this is all mere cruci-fiction. It is a suffering as artificial as the intelligence of the same name. All these bodies sacrificed, tormented and martyred in the name of a desire without organs are merely the rewriting of a lost identity: this is my body, this is my blood. But who is speaking? And this is exchanged for what? For nothing. They are bodies sacrificed to the idea of sacrifice. Orlan, Stelarc and all the rest – sacrificial mannequins.

All these psycho-dramaturges of body-art, body-alteration, body-modification (with biurgy and the plastic surgeons of the genome waiting in the wings) are introverts: they set out their own body as a narcissistic territory and strive to exhaust its possibilities, with no other project than this pathetic, clownish inventory. This is the 'umbilical limbo'.[19]

Kafka's 'hunger-artist' was more discreet and heroic in the expropriation of his body. Abandoned like an old dog by the crowds which once applauded him in the fairgrounds, he went on fasting all the same – to death.

You don't go to the exhibition so much to go there as to *have been* there. You visit some faraway places not so much to see them as to *have seen* them. We do a lot of things purely in order to *have done* them. And many undertakings are designed not so much to reach their goal as to be done with their end. 'We did it!'

19. The reference is to Artaud's 1925 text 'L'Ombilic des limbes', translated as 'Umbilical Limbo', in Artaud, *Collected Works*, vol. 1 (Calder, London 1970).

Being alive means retaining the possibility of dying. Whereas the converse is not true. This is why it is better to be alive than dead.

How can we trust people who can't even make their computers restart from the year 2000? How can we trust machines which can't even move on automatically to the next century? The real millennium bug is the mental impossibility of resetting the counters to zero (00) and really moving into a new era. The computers' refusal to play along is merely the technical expression of this.

The first two world wars were in the classical image of war. The first put an end to European supremacy and the colonial era. The second put an end to Nazism. The third, which did take place, in the form of Cold War and deterrence, put an end to Communism. With each succeeding war we have always moved closer to a single world order. Today that world order, which has virtually reached its end, finds itself grappling, in all the current convulsions, with the antagonistic forces spread throughout the global dimension itself. A fractal war of all cells, of all singularities, rebelling in the form of antibodies. A clash so elusive that the idea of war has to be rescued from time to time by spectacular set-pieces like the Gulf War.

But the fourth world war is going on elsewhere. It is the only truly world war, since what is at stake is globalization itself. And its end will be the catastrophic collapse of World Order and of universal values in general.

Seen my native city again thirty or forty years on. Mind-boggling precision of the memory of places, names and situations. Resurgence of tiny details. Everything is registered, undyingly, in the convolutions of the brain. And, at the same time, absence of any real emotion. You meditate at the sites of your childhood with the same indifference as you do beside your own tomb.

Fukuyama is right about the imposture of European intellectuals. They make reference to Nietzsche, Bataille, Sade or Artaud, while adhering to a democratic morality which absolutely contradicts the radicality of those writers' analyses. None of these great immoralists would have signed a single one of the petitions doing the rounds today.

What is useful is useful for something. But what is useless – is useless for what? For nothing. But which is the most useful function – the something or the nothing?

Raising theory to its state of grace, where, without being imposture (in its relation to truth), it can pass for a stratagem (in its relation to the world).

When the nothing is exchanged for the Nothing, under the sign of the general equivalence of the Nothing, that is the final stage of political economy.

The One has no meaning. It is an abstract, unintelligible entity. One thing is nothing. One single person is no one.

Eins ist keins. Einer ist keiner.

The modern woman is faced with a strange dilemma: power or seduction. Couldn't she have both at the same time? But why would she have this privilege? Long before women, men paid the price for the 'manly' principle of domination. They were the first to sacrifice seduction on the altar of power, along with many other qualities – which women are currently losing by going down the same path.

Heat is a dark room in which the body savours the slow death throes of its cells.

A friend has died. The death of a friend finds its own justification a posteriori: it makes the world less liveable, and therefore renders his absence from this world less painful. It alters the world in such a way that he would no longer have his place in it. Others outlive themselves into a world which is no longer theirs. Some know how to slip away at the apposite moment. Their death is a stroke of cleverness: it makes the world more enigmatic, more difficult to understand than it was when they were alive – which is the true task of thought.

As for Lévi-Strauss, he is immortal. From the depths of his academic immortality he is awaiting the return of the societies with no writing. Perhaps he does not have long to wait. For the coming society, computerized and illiterate, will also be a society without writing. It is our future primitive society.

It is not we who are ageing, but time. It is ageing even more quickly than we are. Does it know this? But it seems in a hurry to come to an end. At all events, we shall all die infinitely young.

COOL MEMORIES IV: 1995-2000

Let us stop imputing our actions to some objective cause, which amounts to saying we have no part in what happens to us. An idea which is downright humiliating. Let us accept the hypothesis that our misfortunes derive from an evil genius that is our own. Let us be worthy of our perversity, of our propensity for evil; let us be equal to our tragic imbecility.

'God is nonexistent' does not mean that He does not exist, but that His existence has no decisive impact on the course of events. We may speak of the political class as nonexistent in this same way. This means that even its uselessness has no appreciable impact on the course of our lives.

Might the cerebral development of the human race be linked to the primal crime (Jean-Pierre Changeux)? The act on which the exponential development of human faculties is established is the primal crime. The act which establishes otherness is the murder of one's fellow.

In inventing the ceaseless light of information, as rival to the original light of the universe, we dream in fact of re-creating the conditions of the Big Bang, which is merely the projection of our current technologies and their secret fantasy of ultimate disintegration. We make it a limiting past event only because we dream of reproducing it. *Punto primal, punto final.*

From gravity we get an energy that is at least the equal of the energy from the sun's rays. Organic beings are bound to their centres of gravity as they are to the centre of the earth, and we play on this perpetual falling of bodies in all our movements. It is as a consequence of time's inertia that things continue in being; otherwise, they would vanish in real time. Unfortunately, it is one of the phantasms of science to abolish gravity and one day, inevitably, technology will 'release' us from this natural law of bodies – into a new physics of virtual bodies. In the future habitat of orbital capsules, we shall no longer even stand upright. What will human intelligence be like then?

Anything to do with the velocipede is of a pataphysical order (it always makes you think of Jarry). But the finest *objet introuvable* remains the tandem – irresistibly evoking the image of two cyclists, back-to-back or face-to-face, pedalling frantically in opposite directions and marking time at a tremendous lick.[20]

A prophet is not without honour, save in his own country. And this goes even more for those who live in exile. And yet more for those who live in internal exile.

To be a mirror, but a two-way mirror: to see others from behind the screen of one's own persona.

20. Jacques Carelman's *Catalogue des objets introuvables* was translated into English by Rosaleen Walsh. For the machines to which Baudrillard seems to be referring here ('K1. Converging tandem' and 'K2. Divergent tandem'), see Carelman, *Catalogue of Extraordinary Objects* (Abelard-Shuman, London 1971), p. 66.

'. . . that absurd sculpture by Picasso, with its stalks and leaves of metal; neither wings, nor victory, just a testimony, a vestige – the idea, nothing more, of a work of art. Very similar to the other ideas and vestiges that inspire our existence – not apples, but the idea, the reconstruction by the pomologist of what apples used to be – not ice-cream, but the idea, the memory of something delicious, made from substitutes, from starch, glucose and other chemicals – not sex, but the idea or evocation of sex – the same with love, belief, thought and the rest . . .'[21]

Dinner for E.O. on his induction into the Académie Française. All his women are there. I had the same idea myself, but done posthumously: seeing all the women in your life walking in silence before your coffin. The finest of celebrations, but only when it is done posthumously. E.O. has clearly understood this, as election to the Académie is the equivalent of a first-class funeral.

Writing is vulgar
Travel is so common
Speaking is obscene
Thinking is too easy
And making love is dated
There remains the possibility of inscribing mnemonic signs, above and beyond the conscious amnesia, in the insignificant verbum of current minds, the figures

21. This passage is cited from an unidentified work by Saul Bellow, and I have not been able to trace the original. As a result, I can only offer here a retranslation of the French.

of melancholia and the fine arts in which hyper-knowledge melds with being-for-the-void – a diacritical representation which, in itself, sets conceptual postulates a-signifying, jostling with the plenitude of a posthumous grace and, *in extremis*, with the absolute void and the figure of the glaciation of the concept.

Just like dogs, who are indifferent to cars but bark fiercely at anyone on foot, seagulls are unmoved by the ear-splitting passage of jets, but the slightest human presence whips up a storm of strident cries. It is, in fact, humans alone they fear. They alone are the enemy. And it is no different with human beings themselves: they can be assailed by all kinds of things, but it is against their fellow men that they mobilize.

It is on the days when the wind comes from the sea, on misty, damp days, that you most expect to see Hannibal's elephants passing the *bergerie*, travelling along the Via Domitiana from Spain to Rome to lay waste to it.

Censorship makes it possible to conceal the worthlessness of a book or an artwork. Quite a bit of art has travelled under cover of censorship, of repression or simulated provocation, which serve it as diplomatic bag and false advertising. Now that this curse has been lifted, art appears in all its insignificance.

Masterpieces bore us with their sacred conformism. You end up preferring the interchangeable lesser masters, painters of impeccable technique and refinement, the almost ritualistic, decorative art of the countless Flemish landscapes, of nineteenth-century portraits, *trompe-l'œil* works and Chinese prints. It seems that, once the proud wind of history has blown itself out, the mystery which remains is that of the obscure works, most of which have disappeared.

Before a congregation not greatly fired with the spirit of sacrifice, the parish priest makes his plea: 'Be like Christ – suffering, crucified, but risen!' And what would these people do with a resurrection, since they do not even know what meaning to give to their present lives? A subtle parable follows: Christ calls on the Apostles not to reveal that he is the Messiah, for, he says, the Jews want only one thing of the Messiah: that he make their hens lay ten times a day (this is exactly how these parishioners think, too). Then he stigmatizes the Whites of the Sahel region (where he once lived) for grabbing all the food for themselves during a famine and throwing the leftovers to the locals (who, among the congregation, would not have done the same?).

Lastly, to sensitize them to misfortune, he tells the story of a young man from the next village whose mother and brother died in a road accident, whose father killed himself while handling his hunting rifle, and who committed suicide at thirty-three – a story which clearly exceeds their capacity for compassion. Yet you feel that the people here don't need things spelling out, and have their own ideas about these things.

And there are indeed some strange characters among the congregation. The young woman with close-cropped, dark hair in the red dress – an adulterous creature if ever there was one. And this innocent young girl leaning over her father, who seems much too affectionate towards her – the mother is praying to be pardoned for her indulgence. Foolish and a little nervous, the adolescent with the delicate neck mumbles her creed half-heartedly.

All the innermost recesses of the soul are to be found in these church pews. They all like their priest and do as they want with their lives.

The blood-red colour of the salt beds, which turns in one sunny afternoon to the pink-striped white of a field of snow. The geometric pattern of the salt works adds a completely unreal dimension to the horizon of oil refineries with the oil tankers lying at anchor off the ponds – ponds against which a fleet of lorries and excavators flit to and fro. The pale red brine gives the impression of a dead solution, or of menstrual blood. One's very gaze liquefies as it slides over this surface, and the body becomes lost in the contemplation of its own fluid. It feels as though one were reliving the events of what was the first crystallization, then by foetal transfusion the emergence of blood, of life, of mother-liquor, in a solution both chemical and maternal.

The sky is an intense blue. In the distance the sea is green and grey. Only black is missing. The only black in nature is shadow and here, on the salt works, there are no shadows.

Orwell: 'There are quite enough real causes of trouble already, and we need not add to them by encouraging young men to kick each other on the shins amid the roars of infuriated spectators.'[22] But the point is precisely this: sporting violence does not superadd itself to real troubles, it eclipses them by diversion into an imaginary

22. George Orwell, 'The Sporting Spirit', in *The Collected Essays, Journalism and Letters*, vol. 4 (Penguin Books in Association with Martin Secker and Warburg, London 1970), p. 64. First published in *Tribune*, 14 December 1945.

violence. So, with football and the World Cup we see sport stealing the power to generate national cohesion from the political sphere. The whole of the political dimension has now shifted into the stadia, as the destiny of the Byzantine Empire once shifted on to the results of the races in the Hippodrome. A fine lesson for those in power, who are only too happy to see football bear the hellish burden of responsibility for mystifying the masses.

Feminists see the slightest hint of seduction as an act of violence. There are others who think that fellatio isn't a sexual act (Clinton). Each version as absurd as the other. Yet what they enable us to glimpse is that, to our frightened sensibilities, all signs have become harassment; whereas for our extenuated moralities, all acts have less and less significance.

Perfect egoism is very rare. The will to power is very rare. Stirner and Nietzsche's imperatives are almost inaccessible. Even the instinct of self-preservation is a chimera. The theory that man is selfish by nature is true only at the 'economic' level (if then), but in other respects the distinction between self and others does not exist. We act towards ourselves with the same cynicism, the same affection, the same forms of seduction and repulsion, destruction and appropriation as we act towards others – in a word, with the same alteregoism. The individual does himself exactly as much harm – with just as much pleasure – as he does to others. In this sense, he is quite unprejudiced. The human race itself, as a whole, with the technical servitude and cruelty it inflicts on itself, treats itself no better – acting without privilege or prejudice – than it treats primitives or animals. Perhaps it is even planning to inflict on itself, in roundabout ways, the same extermination as the one to which it slowly but surely dooms all other races.

On the principle that, in a weakened body, virulence decreases, the practices of bloodletting and fasting were not so bad from the health angle. No worse than the practices of asceticism or mortification from the moral angle.

When the sexual function flickers, as if about to go out, like the vital-function indicators of Hal, the computer in *2001* – or the stars extinguished one by one in Clarke's story.[23] Desire pales like the moon in the early-morning light.

Turning poverty and violence into leitmotivs of advertising, as Toscani does; reincorporating AIDS, sex, war and death into fashion – why not? The advertising vision of happiness is no less obscene. But on one condition: it must show the violence of advertising itself, the violence of fashion, the violence of the medium. Something advertisers are wholly incapable of. Now, the fashionable world itself – the faces of the stars, the underwater dance routines – are a spectacle of death. The world's woes are just as readable in the figure and face of a model as in the skeletal body of an African. You can read the same cruelty everywhere if you know how to see it.

23. Arthur C. Clarke, 'The Nine Billion Names of God', in *Of Time and Stars* (Roc, Harmondsworth 1992), pp. 15–23.

For the criminal, the thing most to be feared is the temptation to confess his crime. For the crime to be perfect, then, it has to be wiped from the murderer's mind by a kind of mental cleansing not unlike the illusion which leads others spontaneously to accuse themselves of crimes they have not committed.

These are extreme cases. But deep down in everyone's consciousness there is no more objective truth than there is in facts – these latter becoming lost in the meanders of narrative and memory. For example, in the Simpson trial in California and in the Omar trial ('Omar m'a tuer'),[24] we have seen the truth pass into a state beyond our reach, as the investigations have proceeded. The time of the action and the time of the trial are no longer the same, and the clear consciousness of the act has been lost. It is likely that neither Simpson nor Omar now really knows whether he committed the crime. And in that state, no lie detector can reach them.

Reality is like 'day for night' – the night scenes shot in daylight – or the effect of actions we perform in another dimension, like the bottle knocked over by a sudden movement, which was merely a movement in a dream.

24 In 1994 Omar Raddad, a gardener at Mougins (Alpes-Maritimes), was convicted of the murder of Mme Ghislaine Marchal, who, according to the prosecution, had scrawled the words 'Omar m'a tuer' [sic] in her own blood on the door of the wine cellar before expiring. The grammatical error in this bizarre message, together with other elements of the case, cast considerable doubt on the verdict from a very early stage. In September 1998 Raddad was freed, after receiving a partial presidential pardon. A DNA analysis carried out in February 2001 on blood found elsewhere at the scene seems further to indicate that the Moroccan was probably not the murderer.

Unlike the theoretical and mental landscape, which is continually shrinking, the landscape of the world and appearances is constantly becoming more diverse. It is difficult to be surprised in the world of ideas, difficult not to be by the perpetual play of forms.

The substance of vampires, like that of ectoplasms and perverse creatures, is so light that it leaves no mark on film. Like the man who had to pass the same way twice to cast a shadow.

'Without the passions, the soul would have no grounds whatever to remain joined to the body' (Descartes).

Ultimately, the critics stigmatize Netanyahu only because he discredits Israel and puts at risk its moral authority, which provides the ultimate basis of its state power. The oppression and spiritual torment of the Palestinians don't come into it. (It can't be long before we see them accused of being, by their very existence, the agents of this moral and political degradation of Israel.) We find the same ambiguity on the part of officers of the law towards the politicians they investigate: their condemnations merely reinforce the moral underpinnings of a domination put at risk by the dominators themselves.

What made a crucial difference in the contaminated-blood affair was the prejudiced belief that a charitable donor is necessarily someone of unimpeachable morality and, for that reason, could not be suspected of killing anyone, even unwittingly.

Secondary-school pupils are demanding more school, more funding, more staff, more security. Nineteenth-century demands. School is finished. All we can do is transform it into a gigantic Web café. In their own heads, the school students have already moved over into multimedia and the twenty-first century, as is attested by the incongruity of the demonstrations, including the incongruity of the anachronistic violence of the hooligan element.

We reply to the perpetual calls on us by a kind of automatic erasure. First it is proper names, then titles, figures, formulae, then even faces and histories, and ultimately one's own name and code number. We wipe all these the way we forget a dream when we wake, or the way a cassette destroys itself in real time. By blanking out the film of real life, we blank out the film of mental life. There's nothing on the film any more. Blank, white. Ethnic cleansing of the memory.

Generally speaking, rights are as stupid as the prohibitions they replace. But the worst thing is casting in terms of law and rights situations which had no need of it – a right to water, a right to air, a right to desire, children's right to have parents. This legal recognition creates the most ludicrous contradictions, such as the condemned prisoner whom the 'right-to-life' activists want to have pardoned, but who demands to be executed in the name of his right to die.

And what are we to say of this 'right to life'? Other than that it makes the point very well: *de jure* life is life that has lost its *de facto* obviousness.

Rights, then, function as exorcism, as a desperate invocation of lost qualities.

Given the current spread of stupidity, no doubt we shall soon be seeing the emergence of a 'right to intelligence'.

The international polluter's permit: is each country to have its legal allocation of CO_2, with the polluting countries being allowed to buy up the shares of the non-polluting ones? This way the United States, by buying up Russia's 'pollution entitlement', could fund an economic boom which would allow the Russian economy to get back to polluting again. We might even envisage a black market in which the non-polluters would sell back their carbon monoxide quota at a semi-official world rate, like any other kind of commodity. The same scenario as for world debt – being sold on, and quoted on the stock market. You can never cease to marvel at the market's absolute indifference to the nature of goods. Even carbon monoxide can now be traded freely.

The fateful consequence of the Clinton affair – sexuality banalized as a murky relationship of infantile gropings – is not political. It is transpolitical, and it is derision on a world scale. Seen in the deriding of Clinton, to begin with: how can he bear such clownishness? And the clownishness, too, of a whole culture capable of producing such a spectacle. Not just American, but planetary culture – the planet finally globalized through ridicule and derision. No other culture could have borne such a degree of abasement without triggering some mechanism of reparative violence. The fact that this scenario has not given rise to a universal sense of revulsion attests to a considerable raising of the threshold of our tolerance of the very worst.

Instead of talking about 'animal rights' and dreaming of a multiculturalism of species, let us remember that animals are gods and that, in the past, they were sacrificed as such; that they were regarded as superior both in strength and in beauty; and that they were in collusion with us. That is to say: they were our forebears and fellows in the cycle of metamorphoses, not our vulgar predecessors in the line of evolution (we have done them the honour of being descended from them, but that was not what they asked). We did not feel despair at resembling animals. Indeed, we took on animal masks (up to the Lascaux figures, bestiality is a mask, and all our masks are the masks of bestiality), since they were the living memory of our passage into the realms of inhumanity – and we respected even their silence, which was itself the living memory of our passage through original silence.

Putting an end to millions of years of man's mingling with water, mud, vegetation and dust, we are currently burying the soil, the base on which we stand, in an enormous shroud of asphalt and concrete, much as we bury mutual human closeness in a shroud of information and communication.

There are so many signs of happiness here (in Brazil), and so many signs of unhappiness. They are often the same, and one learns not to distinguish between them.

Palacio Itamarati. All the gentry of Rio surrounded by the tropical downpour in a palace worthy of Caracalla – the columns of the porticos competing with the fluorescent palms, and the swans on the lake indifferent beneath the deluge. Remake of *The Exterminating Angel*. Thousands of guests at the Biennale, all of them of rare elegance, scattered around the immense halls. The last women arrive, their dresses streaming with rain. The downpour seems to have hit the palace particularly heavily. The other parts of the city have been spared. Is this God's judgement on the usurpation for cultural purposes of what was previously a shrine to power?

Norway. In the cold and the silence, the visual field empties. Sounds, on the other hand, are strikingly close. Nostalgia for a primal nature, an imageless depth, a depth without signs as far as the eye can see. This very soon becomes unbearable: it is in the artificial and the superficial that we are like fish in water.

The Osiris lounge for first-class passengers (there is a certain irony in giving the luxury lounge the name of an Egyptian divinity who presided over the judgement of the dead, and whose body was dismembered[25] before it was resuscitated). Champagne, silence, distance – the anteroom of death. Everyone spreads out as far as possible from the others, like the souls of the dead wandering about beyond the Styx without touching or seeing each other. However, an atmosphere of international pimping prevails, not unrelated to the ringing of mobile phones.

But what do we know of the proxemics of the dead and their social behaviour? Do they even have space? And, where the rich and their places of luxury are concerned, are we not already in a funerary field of sensory isolation, which the poor,

25. By Seth, his brother.

who seem less allergic to the proximity of their fellow man, might be said so far to have escaped?

How can you dream about an earthquake at 10,000 metres? How can you dream with such staggering precision the mechanics of a catastrophe you have never really experienced?

How can you live and relive in a dream, with such divinatory intuition, the acts, words and expressions of someone else – play his role better than he does in reality?

The heroes of humanitarian action are applauded: a good thing they're there to rescue our honour! If you denounce this shroud-waving, again there is applause: thank goodness you're there to say these things! It is often the same people who applaud. Sycophants, catechumens, proselytes, acolytes – to arms, all of you!

Irresponsibility is presented as a natural inclination, responsibility as a conscious act. But this is not the case at all. Responsibility – the mere fact of responding – is a reflex act. It is when it becomes a rule of conscience that it is oppressive. Then it must be compensated by the equally vital faculty of not responding. There is a duty of irresponsibility equal to the duty of responsibility, particularly in the current climate, when we are constantly being tested, called upon, harassed. Irresponsibility, like all good charity, begins at home. You have to know how not to be responsible for what does not concern you, and this goes for things in your own life too. The

Stoics' distinction between what is our concern and what is not remains the alpha and omega of a philosophical morality.

The man with his mobile phone steps over the threshold of the exhibition. His phone rings. He goes right round the exhibition without a glance, riveted as he is to his inner ear. He speaks, and looks at you as though you were on the other end of the line. He is looking at someone he is not speaking to. He is talking to someone he cannot see. Purposeless purpose of the wire-less phone.

Thought is not a matter of time or accumulation. It's no use heating water to 80 degrees for hours. It won't come to the boil. All it will ever do is evaporate.

Isn't being passive allowing the other part of yourself to take the initiative? Nabokov: 'He loved himself with a love that was passionate . . . and requited.' Stanislav Lec: 'He loved himself very much, but his sentiments were not reciprocated.'

'People of good taste leave it to the common herd to think, and to think wrongly' (Crébillon). That same aristocratic position is today occupied by the common herd, who leave it to the politicians to govern us, and to govern us badly. The mediocre have turned the tables.

Exoteric machines – esoteric machines.
    They say the computer is an improved form of typewriter. Not a bit of it. I

collude with my typewriter, but the relationship is otherwise clear and distant. I know it is a machine; it knows it is a machine. There is nothing here of the inter-face, verging on biological confusion, between a computer thinking it is a brain and me thinking I am a computer.

The same familiarity with good old television, where I was and remained a spec-tator. It was an esoteric machine, whose status as machine I respected. Nothing there of all these screens and interactive devices, including the 'smart' car of the future and the 'smart' house. Even the mobile phone, that incrustation of the net-work in your head, even the skateboard and rollerblades – mobility aids – are of a quite different generation from the good old static telephone or the velocipedic machine. New manners and a new morality are emerging as a result of this organic confusion between man and his prostheses – a confusion which puts an end to the instrumental pact and the integrity of the machine itself.

A woman is beautiful only if she is naked beneath her clothes. A thought is beau-tiful only if it is naked beneath language. In other words, violent. Each sentence is the spark of a will to power.

Regency of the Instincts and Death Throes of the Emotions.

The tendency to laziness, or quite simply the inclination to turn one's back on obligations or complications of all kinds, is countered by an even more tenacious fault: the tendency to respond to every demand, such as, for example, always to arrive on time. It would be so much simpler to be neither the one nor the other:

neither lazy nor impatient. But the obsession with the deadline is always there. You would like everything to be there from the very outset and, at the same time, everything to be postponed indefinitely.

With Parity,[26] International Women's Day and, more recently, the Chiennes de Garde,[27] and, more generally, with every claim to victimal difference, women are making themselves a collective laughing stock, alongside gays, with their demand for a bourgeois, legal, marital status.

Exophthalmia – or having eyes larger than your head
Trichotomy – or the art of splitting hairs
Xylolalia – or the language of political cliché
Taxidermy – or the art of embalming concepts alive.

'Les Hommes': a sloppy, charmless, tedious theatricality. Improvisation which is unscrupulous, yet heavily allegorical: an allegory of an emptiness which aims to signify that it has understood everything and is fooled by nothing. What has happened for us to have gone from the tragic, metaphysical expression of emptiness – that of Beckett – to the emptiness of any old thing?

26. The reference is to the French electoral law, which requires parties to produce balanced candidate lists or run the risk of losing part of their state funding.
27. 'Les Chiennes de Garde' is a feminist organization committed to supporting women in public life.

The infantile mania for depraving language in journalistic style, for exploiting it with puns, as though it were a faecal object, for cultivating a clownish rhetoric.

The opposite mania, brought on by an etymological obsession, for sacrificing language to textuality, by forcing words to confess their unconscious genesis, as others do with the sexual unconscious.

Rothko says that his pictures have two characteristics: either they dilate and then open up in all directions, or they contract and then close up precipitately on all sides. Between these two poles lies everything he has to say.

Rothko's change, his passage almost without transition, to an immediate, definitive form. It is there all at once, perfectly mastered, end of story. And it is light-years from what he was doing up to that point.

This is something entirely different from an evolution – even a creative evolution. It is an almost genetic impulse by which he separates himself miraculously from the artist he still was, with his place in the history of art, to be nothing but the sovereign medium of an extremely simple form, which no longer has anything to do with expressionism or abstraction.

'The emergent form stuns you with its simplicity. And perhaps the most surprising thing is that, during our earthly existence, in which our brains are bound with bands of steel – the tightly-fitting dream of our own personality – we did not by chance give that little mental shake which would have freed the imprisoned thought and procured for it the ultimate understanding' (Nabokov).

Does not everyone have in them this potential mutation, this potential development? This absolute singularity which asks only to be effortlessly produced – 'an inspired form that has sloughed off our individual yoke'?

The almost timeless curvature of the space of ideas obeys neither chronology nor history. So the thoughts of Sade and Fourier are like anticipated repercussions of the theories of Marx and Freud, of which they are a much more radical critique *avant la lettre* than any that were to follow, exerting their effects only posthumously. To reread the world of ideas against the grain of the ideology of the Enlightenment, the ideology of a chronological order of events.

Finalistic, moral vision which leads François Furet to distinguish between the good and bad events of the French Revolution, and to stigmatize the Terror, attesting to an inability to grasp what, in the event, exceeds objective (initial or final) conditions at the cost of a violence against itself on the part of the event. Thermidorians know nothing of Messidor.

Ceronetti: 'If I thought my justice was tending to delay the collapse of things, I would strive to be a little less just.'

Freedom is not as free as is generally thought: it produces antibodies which rebel against it. Truth, too, is threatened from within, like a state battling with its own police force. If values enjoyed total immunity, they would be as lethal as a scientific truth.

If language makes the human being an unnatural social and cultural animal, that fact is balanced out by it being language, too, which enables him to lie, and hence to bear that abnormal condition.

Our most ordinary perception obeys a kind of aesthetic protocol which states that there must always be something to see and someone to see it. In other cultures, only a few rare things are presented to the gaze. The rest is suprasensible, and eludes both aesthetics and culture. It is when this rule is abolished that the world is given over to a universal protocol of sensibility, in which the very appearance of things is converted into a cultural value.

One always has the impression that other people's existences should have a meaning – unlike our own, which we live as a dramatic exception to the general happiness or discontent. How do they manage to live lives that are so worthless, so wearisome? But we would none the less like to slip into this mediocrity in order to learn the secret of it.

In purely democratic terms, the surrealistic inculpation of Clinton for an act of fellatio is an absolute advance over the impunity men in power generally enjoy. On the other hand, in terms of transparency and information, one has to say that it opens on to an abyss of derision and obscenity for which the sexual affair is merely an allegory.

The only alternative to getting rid of the Rio *favelas* would be to make them part of World Heritage – an ideal solution for all threatened species and places. Ultimately, the only solution for the planet itself: making it part of World Heritage – along with the human genome.

Waiting is like an anticipated expiation – something we have to pay the price for in advance (including waiting for death?). Impatience provides the counter to this – as an immediate demand for the end.

In a society given over to the principle of Evil, there is no presumption of innocence. Asthma, an ulcer, an allergy, acne, tinnitus – all these things testify against you. Even cancer and coronaries are psychologically suspect. Even accidents. By the same token, medicine becomes suspect too, since it operates on the borders of a phantom pathology, where 'organic' disorders are overdetermined by bad conscience or bad faith. What is too shameful to mention now is not sex, but the psyche, or rather the mental disorder which gives rise to this non-compliance of the body – illnesses that are no longer sexually but psychologically shameful, contracted through a guilty relationship with . . . reality.

The true 'break of the age'[28] is when it becomes clear – against the vital illusion of a 'resumption' (Kierkegaard), especially of amorous relations, where the second

28. In English in the original.

encounter would be the ideal *dénouement* – that this sublime repetition will definitively not take place. No recall, no return, no second existence. Everything then becomes suddenly mortal.

The faintest glimmer of intelligence among those in power can only add to the calamity, just as truth can only aggravate matters. Better cynicism and corruption. They at least form part of objective conditions, of which the side that is in the light is turned towards evil.

Society debased itself by shooting the mutineers of 1917. It is debasing itself a second time by rehabilitating them. And it debases them too, once and for all, for surely those who died on the field of dishonour have the right to stay there. Let us not revive them on the field of honour, which is tantamount to spitting on their graves (not to mention that those rehabilitating them today would, in the past, have shot them just the same).

This is how the victims are swept away, together with the moral superiority they had as victims. This is how their revenge is stolen from them (while they are still secretly regarded as guilty). Let us leave the mutineers, the rebels, the outcasts and the accursed their privilege of the 'accursed share'. Let us not have the victimizers usurp their place by the staging of confessions and repentance.

The same scenario with the Church and the victims of the Inquisition: the implication here is that these forms of persecution, blackmail and terror are finished, whereas others, much more universal and subtle in character, are developing – forms we cannot even imagine being contested.

With Pinochet, Papon, Saddam and Milošević, with all those who have served as mercenaries for the 'international community', it is impossible for that community to disown them openly. It can only spirit them away beneath more or less rigged trials. And, just as it goes on regarding the victims as secretly guilty, it continues to regard *them* as secretly innocent.

The Evian advert. The waltz of the water babies, metaphor for spermatozoa wriggling around in uterine plasma. The larval babies soaring up from the charnel house of their birth.[29] The mawkishness of these pre-pubescent, pre-natal, infantile advertisements – positive obscenity of an adult world. *Pampers* culture. You end up feeling nostalgic for the golden age of woman as sex-object and for eroticism in advertising.

PACS,[30] CAP,[31] Parity, etc.: a general chemotherapy for dying functions, for everything which finds itself expelled by the violent rationalization of the social body – the family, the rural world – in conformity with an aerodynamic profile of social exchanges.

29. 'hors du charnier natal'. The phrase is from Hérédia's poem 'Les Conquérants': 'Comme un vol de gerfauts hors du charnier natal', the 'charnel house' in question presumably being the nest of the predatory gyrfalcons, doubtless littered with bones.
30. The 'Pacte civile de solidarité', which is sometimes interpreted as 'gay marriage'.
31. Common Agricultural Policy.

The extraordinary levitation of dreams, which carries me above the roofs and the city, takes me through walls like an ectoplasm, then has me swoop like a bird on its prey and break in on the most intimate spaces – including the women you caress with impunity. Your hands plunge beneath any dress, catching unawares a woman trembling beneath caresses from she knows not where. Pleasure in the immaterial world is more intense than in reality, but where does it come from? In the world of dreams, nothing ever seems to age. Sensations are always as intense as ever. Will virtual reality and the electronic promiscuity of the networks offer such remote sensations, this same capacity to pass through walls and caress 'sleeping beauties'?

I always arrive on time, a thing which reflects the punctuality of our rendezvous with death, when we can only ever be precisely on time. Or, rather, it is death which will be right on time, come what may. Not that it is waiting for us. It just happens that when it is there, we shall be there too. And that is how it should be. The worrying (mortifying?) thing is the anticipation of this inexorable coincidence by arriving on time where punctuality has little importance. After all, those who never arrive on time are merely playing with a 'time-delayed' death. Now, our entire culture has trained us over centuries in this obsessive punctuality, and hence for the rendezvous with death. The only way we have found of escaping it is 'real time', the dispersal of time into the perpetual interface, so that there is no precise point where death could be there right on time.

Some thoughts can arise simultaneously in more than one brain, just as the human species emerged simultaneously in more than one region of the globe. Or is it a case

90

of ideas sliding around within a single brain, shared by certain persons at a particular moment – like that 40,000-tree forest in the north of Canada all joined together, constituting one immense organic being? However that may be, nothing is more disturbing than a thought being expressed by someone else at the very moment it is being born in your head – like the advance, muted echo of a piece of music before the orchestra actually strikes up.

The melancholy of analysis and the analytic superego. The theoretical object finds it harder and harder to regenerate itself through the play of truth.

The photographic object, by contrast, regenerates of itself through the play of appearances – no more superego, no more analysis, no more melancholy.

The photographic object is apocatabasic.

If reality is our stock in trade, then Virtual Reality is the equivalent of the hyper-market.

Isn't the photogenic polite smile a defensive mask, a way of playing dead to escape the predator?

Language, too, has its molars for grinding, its incisors for cutting, its canines for tearing – and, from time to time, a wisdom tooth.

Silence is a property of images. But that silence is merely the stilling of the voice. Most images howl in another way. They howl with truth and reality.

Aesthetic lifting of faces.
Ethical face-lifting of values.
Genetic face-lifting of the genome.
Mental face-lifting of ideas.

Jeff Koons: impossible to know whether he is stupid or not, whether he can distinguish the kitsch from the original, the true from the false. He is pure simulacrum, steeped in a total innocence, either ironic or 'zero-degree'. Beneath an angelic, infantile exterior, he is the disenchanted verification, the icy self-evidence of a world of empty signs. Whereas there is, in Warhol, all the charm of simulation – and, above all, the intuitive sense of what it has always been: namely, nothing more than a hypothesis – with Jeff Koons we are at the burlesque stage of simulation as joke or as stereotype. All the same, the simulacrum hypothesis deserved better than to become a reality.

Everything needs a second occurrence, just as the Anabaptists needed a second baptism to exist spiritually. So we should postpone all actions, all decisions, to allow them the possibility of a second baptism.

In all circumstances, the problem is how to be there and not be there – simultaneously. In other words, to be precisely how we are in relation to the world: we are in it and we are not in it.

The sudden cancellation of a planned event or of some decision or other is one of those subtle pleasures with which chance occasionally blesses us.

If destiny is implacable, that is because you have not known how to please it.

The Transphilosophical Divide:[32] the point where truth begins to exist on both sides of the line, the point where all contradictory hypotheses can be simultaneously verified.

You have disappeared. You have passed on. You don't know it right away. You know it when other people's judgements and the perpetual misunderstanding affect you less and less. The caesura has occurred, without any visible event to mark it. You can no longer be reached by the usual channels.

The temptation for torturers and dictators is to treat even more cruelly those whom human rights and Amnesty International protect (virtually). No pity for those minorities. If 'they' have the right to be different, then the only solution is to liquidate them physically. This is the paradoxical consequence of the 'right to difference'. Torture certainly did not wait until the modern age to make its appearance, but it has surely developed an exciting modern variant in the violation not just of human beings, but of human rights.

32. In English in the original. This is an allusion to the notion of the 'continental divide'.

Everything in men's fashion – the models' bodies and bearing, the staging, the 'aura of fashion' – is largely feminized. Fashion is feminine, and that is all there is to it.

It is the converse of the social and political world, where the women who play a significant role all take on male characteristics. Power is masculine, and that is all there is to it.

They can assume a seductive air, but this is femininity as an added 'extra'. Similarly, male models can display the stigmata of the male, but this is masculinity as an added 'extra'.

A mother loses her twenty-year-old son in an accident. She says she will donate the boy's eyes, kidneys and liver on condition that his sperm is saved. This done, she goes looking for a woman (a virtual daughter-in-law) who is prepared to give birth to one or more grandchildren. She gets enthusiastic letters from all over the USA. But the Ethics Committees on Embryos point out that she does not have the right to have a dead man produce children. She argues, together with her lawyer, that if the doctors can accept his entrails, then she has the right to do what she wants with her dead son's deep-frozen spermatozoa.

Might it be the destiny of the human race to disappear into a very highly diluted reality, into an irresistible abstraction – a fatal consequence of the irruption of thought? One day we shall no longer understand anything about anything, but there won't be anything to understand – the entire universe will have become information. An immaterial involution. Aphanisis. The end of the show. The species become translucent to itself. A cosmic precedent: the separation of light – the world becomes visible. Second mutation: the separation of thought – the world becomes intelligible. Third phase: it disappears?

Nabokov: 'Being aware of being aware of being. . . . In that respect, the gap between ape and man is immeasurably greater than the one between amoeba and ape.'[33] But how far will this evolution go, this increasing reflexiveness of consciousness? We are already in a four-dimensional consciousness (the first three being the dimensions of representation). Will there be a five-, six- or seven-dimensional consciousness? Which would know that it knows that it knows?

On the eight-lane highways, the thousands of automobiles winding along the hillsides like migrating animals, with all their lights on, as though there were no natural daylight, or as though the headlights were trying to penetrate the mask of another night – peopled with phosphorescent-eyed imagos and spectres, which daylight alone had not managed to dissipate. The same number of cars in each direction – a gigantic zero-sum parade – the same uninterrupted blood-flow, all moving along the same track the same distance from the car in front and the one behind.

33. V. Nabokov, *Strong Opinions* (Vintage International, New York 1990), p. 142.

The days here begin with twilight, with the Pacific mists which create a vaguely Neolithic atmosphere. Then humanity makes its appearance, along the beaches, in the form of the jogger, perfect in his role as prehistoric animal. Then the mists clear, leaving the first swimming pools and the grey-green or turquoise neon lights to sparkle. Then a pastel light, always veiled at this time of year, engulfs this sluggish world, a world benumbed by ease, a world fluid like the thousands of somnambulant cars which pass along endlessly night and day. Finally, the day, which began in a crepuscular daybreak, ends on the dazzling dawning of the setting sun – with all the mist now at last dispersed – like an explosion of volcanic dust.

California: the only authentic Disneyland. The only place in the world where the simulacrum is a home-grown product. All the rest is Disneyfied, but Southern California remains the cradle of hyperreality, the capital of nowhere-land.

In Europe, it seems to be male homosexuality that rules the roost culturally and politically, given the way the legal regulation of mores has developed. In the USA, it is female homosexuality which exerts most pressure and has a predominant influence – to a point of real discrimination. All the business of multiculturalism, 'political correctness' and sexual harassment revolves around this axis, and the triumph of 'gender' is a female homosexual triumph. The problem is whether what is presented as the high point of the evolution of social mores, and which, under cover of multiculturalism, operates as an unchallenged orthodoxy, is not in fact the most advanced stage of the involution of a society towards a co-gender coalition, on the basis of a single, dominant sexual or cultural criterion. The same question can be asked of practices such as surfing the Web, the Internet and all the rest – incestuous niches where everyone ends up geared to the same software and the same programmes, obeying the same technical and mental imperative.

Art dies with inbreeding. This is not unlike the story of mad-cow disease and the animal feeds – live animals being made to eat pulverized dead ones. Art has, in this same way, begun to live off its own pulverized feed, a residue of old forms and of a diligently freeze-dried art history. Most importantly, art has devoured its own idea, or has been devoured by it – an incestuous autophagy, combined with a recycling of its own excrement for internal use.

Intellectuals and politicians are members of a single elite, a single caste with caste privileges. And the discrimination in this case is even worse than it is in traditional societies, since, unlike classical aristocracies, this one cloaks itself in the universal to protect its privileges. Sheltering beneath this symbolic jurisdiction, intellectuals and politicians draw illusory distinctions between themselves just to keep the show on the road.

 'Community of thought, which is the basic bond between men, does not exist in this society' (Michelet).

You become stupid as soon as you lose the ability to imagine stupidity. Even intelligence, if it loses the ability to imagine itself, becomes stupid. So artificial intelligence, which has no ability to imagine its knowledge, however vast, is on a level with the apes.

In *True Crime*, Clint Eastwood shows us an execution by lethal injection. The condemned man is strapped to the operating table (everything is very surgical). The oval room has transparent walls, initially veiled by blinds, behind which sit the family and those who have the privilege of being present at this final scene. The curtains are raised and, as in a real peepshow, the last-minute guests can follow the lengthy official proceedings which precede the orgasm of the three-phase injection. The only difference is that the condemned man can also see those who are watching him, until he falls into a coma: it is an interactive peepshow.

Erik Orsenna attempts to exonerate Jacques Coustaud, whom he succeeds at the Académie Française, from the charge of anti-Semitism by arguing that it was common in France at the time (during the war). Innumerable documents prove that anti-Semitism, avowed or otherwise, was a very widespread attitude. But if there is an accusation worse than that of having been anti-Semitic, it is the accusation of being anti-Semitic when everyone was (or no longer being anti-Semitic when everyone had ceased to be). This is to add a charge of weakness of character to the condemnation of ideas. No one has noticed this.

A book is finished when you think you have taken it as far as you can. That is to say, when you become aware of an insuperable limit which only the book itself can surmount – or, rather, some of its readers, who will carry it to its end and beyond its end. But the sense that the ideal book has escaped you, when it had already long been fully in existence, in a somnambulistic mist from which it merely had to be wrested fragment by fragment – this sense persists, as vital reaction, of an object which, after opening out in its lifetime, now retracts and plays dead, before plunging into a dreamless sleep.

The image is the consecration of everything which, one day or another, must metamorphose to fall silent. It is the finest of the silent metamorphoses of discourse. It is as though discourse had preceded it in a previous life. It retains all the appearances of that, but it has subtly gone over to the other side, to a phenomenal intuition of that of which there is nothing more to be said. Analysis itself, once it has gone to extremes, no longer has a face; it becomes its own mask. It is at that point that it finds a previously unknown element of evidence on the phenomenal side of the image, which, without that analytical intuition, would not exist in the same way.

Leopardi complained about his philosophy of despair and celebration of emptiness being attributed to his misfortunes, deformity and personal misery. Such is the violence of interpretation, which always confuses the principle of evil with the experience of misfortune. And it is, in fact, a double-edged sword, for what value can we attribute to optimistic pronouncements from this standpoint? They would merely be the expression of an equilibrium and a general state of good health – which invalidates them from the viewpoint of meaning and morality. However, Good is never called on to explain itself. It never comes under suspicion of having external motives or reasons too shameful to mention. That is why it is Good: it is not even suspected, and it can rage with impunity.

All the time we used to spend giving meaning to the world is today spent in reproducing it artificially. We gain in this exchange. All the time and energy we used to spend cultivating appearances and pleasures, we now spend transforming the world and exchanging it as value. We lose in that exchange.

All the events which have not taken place, those which got lost on the way, those which were too slow ever to have arrived and other silent ones which will never have had an opportunity to occur – all this makes up the antimatter of our history, the 'missing mass' of absent events which inflects the course of real ones.

Among certain Indians, the placenta is buried or burned at birth, with the same ceremony as is accorded to the dead. The placenta is regarded as a twin of the new-born, as the one sacrificed so that the other may live. For we are always two at the beginning, and the one has to die for the other to live.

We are real only by chance, and immortal without knowing it.

I quote only those I admire, because they managed to say what I wanted to say better than I could. Or said what I feel I could have written. It is like your thought being turned out by someone else, who returns it to you as if you had given it to them. The fact that someone could have thought it before you is a shared sign, a predestined sign, like an object which offers itself to the lens. This pleasure of quotation is, then, extremely rare, and should remain so.

An existence – what is an existence?

Life, existence, 'life stories' – those of Freud and Marx: what they had for break-fast, how they eyed up their maids. The decipherment of thinking by way of trivia, the exegesis of garbage, the biographical 'detective story' which is ravaging the whole of research and literature. The investigation of detail, the infinitesimal existential analysis, in the mad hope of reconstituting the whole – as though all dramaturgy had disappeared from thought and life itself.

If there was once an enchanted moment of the exploration of banality, of the magic of the *fait divers*, of the esotericism of the everyday, it is now the corpse of banality the mercenaries of art are working furiously away on, savouring their own deaths.

At the Ministry of Self-Evidence and Reality, where he was employed on a daily basis as an expert, he had concluded his activities with a report which tended to show that objective facts, objective truths, had always been there – as some philosophies have asserted, and others have denied – but that they were present on a kind of waiting list, and appeared one by one only as space became available, as empty spaces were left by the disappearance of other objective truths. . . .

Ronald Reagan, struck down by Alzheimer's disease, has simply forgotten he was once President of the United States. Is this really so serious? When he was President he had already forgotten he had been an actor. And isn't it more serious to take yourself for the President of the United States when you are, than to forget you have been when you no longer are?

Most of the visitors to Lascaux II don't even know they're visiting the simulacrum of the cave and the wall paintings. There are no longer any signs indicating the whereabouts of the original, which is reserved for a few exceptional visitors. This is a foretaste of the general human condition of the near future: we shall inhabit a world which we no longer know not to be the original. What was merely a philosophical hypothesis will have become a hard reality – but we shall be completely unaware of this.

Why do you go to the café? To observe the madness of others.

Avoid having power over anyone, unless it be the power of life and death.

In a distant country surrounded by water, the people believe the crabs are responsible for the movement of the tides. As they move, the crabs make waves, and as the waves move, they whip up the wind. . . . The Navel of the Waves (Déborah).[34]

Marvellous graffiti on the walls of Bogotá: '*No privatizaron la vida!*' Will life escape global free trade, the destiny of the banks and public institutions? Can it escape deregulation?

34. This appears to be the belief among the nomadic Moken sea-tribe of Thailand. The phrase 'nombril des vagues' appears in 'L'histoire du crabe responsable des marées', as told by Salamah, a member of the Moken.

'*Se prohibe a los materialistas estaçionar en lo absoluto*' (strictly no parking for heavy goods vehicles). But also: no parking for materialists in the absolute! The converse: no parking for idealists in material reality.

The very emergence of individual desire is an infringement of the impersonal norm of the group and the species, of an imprescriptible rule, whatever the benefits of freedom and emancipation. Psychoanalytic 'family conflicts' are merely a limited localization of this symbolic forfeiture of heritage.

With the mobile phone, word no longer passes from mouth to mouth, but from ear to ear. And the ear is no longer the ear of hearing and the voice, but a sensory terminal. A further phase of the electronic colonization of the senses: tactility and the digitality (of screens) substituting for touch; film substituting for the skin; the visual substituting for looking; voice command substituting for the voice, and all the virtual sensors (including erotic ones) substituting for the body and sensuality. Only smell and taste, it seems, have not yet undergone this computer-based metastasis.

Disinterestedness [*gratuité*] is a giving which asks nothing in return. But there is another form of disinterestedness which is a taking without giving anything in return. That, too, is a disinterested act, since it is an act without equivalence, and we should accord it the same dignity. To be able to accept something from someone without any counter-gift on your part – that is to say, to accept someone taking the advantage over you and marking his superiority (this is the symbolic logic of the gift) – is also a sacrifice entirely equivalent to that made by the giver.

The idea of a wind which would blow in all directions at once. A magical idea, like that of a vertical horizon. Thought realizes this idea, signifying as it does in all directions at once. Or the art work in Rothko's conception, which opens up and closes itself off again in all directions at once.

The world does not exist so that we may know it. It is not in any way predestined for knowledge. However, knowledge itself is part of the world, but of the world in its profound illusoriness, which consists in bearing no necessary relation to knowledge.

A well-entrenched obsession or perversion survives a person living beyond his end. The way voodoo man, with an alien spirit riding on his back, no longer has any but a phantom existence, but is carried beyond his end by the incessant presence of the incubus. Like Ahab saying to his trusty carpenter: 'And if I still feel the smart of my crushed leg, though it be now so long dissolved; then, why mayst not thou . . . feel the fiery pains of hell for ever, and without a body? Hah!'[35]

The court of appeal of Huntsville (Texas) has just postponed the execution of a condemned man in order to establish whether he is sane enough to be executed. In the days when we hanged horses (as we still did in the eighteenth century),

35. Herman Melville, *Moby-Dick or the Whale* (Penguin, Harmondsworth 1992), pp. 513–14.

and when punishment was cruel but not sadistic, we did not ask so many questions.

But perhaps it is not even sadistic in the minds of the judges. Perhaps it has quite simply become a human right to be executed in complete awareness of what is going on.

Logically, the mentally deficient should be able to claim an inalienable right to intelligence. The public authorities ought to put an end to this cruel inequality. But no doubt there is hope for them in artificial intelligence.

Psychoanalysis overturned. Instead of the dream being the fulfilment of desires unsatisfied in real life, real life would be the site where desires born of dreams were fulfilled. Instead of being the dumping-ground of the unconscious, dreams would be the matrices of real events – thus becoming like the 'dream' of the Aborigines, for whom a child has to be dreamt before he can be begotten, 'real' paternity being merely the fulfilment of the dream.

Gorbachev to the West: perestroika will come to you too. He was right, but not in a good sense. Once the Berlin Wall had fallen and the spectre of Eastern Europe had disappeared, the respective structures of the two blocs ceased to keep each other in check (which they did not so much by nuclear deterrence as by their internal coherence in the face of the enemy). It was at that point that corruption could develop freely on both sides, and assume global dimensions.

That which one speaks of always has an ironic value – the irony of all discourse. On the other hand, there is a basic obligation towards language. It is because language is more real than what it speaks of that we have the greatest responsibility towards it.

It is not enough that the Church should repent in particular cases – in respect of the Jews, the Latin American Indians, heretics and witches, or Giordano Bruno (what an obscene parody this repentance is! You burned him, let his soul burn in hell!). God Himself should repent, and publicly express His repentance for all the atrocities, mystifications and manipulations practised on humanity over the last two millennia. He will have to be investigated for:

- misuse of spiritual property; use and abuse of debt and grace, fraud and illicit trading in indulgences;
- insider trading (He knows far too much that He has never revealed) and general disinformation through apocryphal gospels;
- formation of armed groups and secret tribunals (the Inquisition);
- construction of buildings to His greater glory out of public funds;
- illegal imprisonment of the Truth, and impersonation – presenting Himself as three persons in one and two natures in one – and for having being so crooked as to spread belief in His own nonexistence (He is, indeed, the biggest creator of Mickey-Mouse jobs who has ever existed);
- absconding: He managed to run off and vanish before the investigation.

As a consequence, the trial will take place in His absence.

He will have no defence counsel. Even Rome takes a poor view of His case.

The sentence: banishment, house arrest, resignation, suicide, incineration and the scattering of His ashes on the Web.

To present woman as an innocent victim of seduction is an insult to femininity itself.

After every natural catastrophe, everyone sets about repairing the damage, without for a moment contemplating, or being staggered by, this heavenly vengeance.

It was an event of such violence that it was impossible not to think that something had taken place elsewhere, and this was merely the extreme consequence of it – more or less the way a ripple from a distant earthquake destroyed the walls of an ancient city at a stroke.

The photographic lens makes you immediately indifferent to yourself – you inwardly play dead. In the same way, the presence of television cameras makes what you are saying seem alien or a matter of indifference.

When some future scientist expresses the idea that the generations of clones and artificial beings that succeed us are descended from man, it will be as terrible a shock as when Darwin announced that man was descended from the apes.

A frosted-glass transparency.

One day we'll discover that the Big Bang didn't take place either. Together with the Y2K bug and all the crashes and clashes, it is one of this century's end's great spectaculars. The end of the century itself is merely a spectacular.

Every refinement of the Western way of life renders it more fragile, and represents a weapon for a potential enemy who has much less to lose. Hence the superiority of the Russians – despite their military inferiority – where the nuclear threat was concerned. Hence the power of the Islamists where suicide is concerned: they make up for their total powerlessness simply with the sacrifice of their lives, whereas on the Western side everything is predicated on 'zero deaths'.

She had an inferiority complex towards herself.

Like the disabled child who sued his mother for not having worn her safety belt, when she was pregnant, in the crash which left him disabled, soon all children will be able to sue their parents for having brought them into the world.

It is from its opposition to something else that something has meaning – it is from its opposition to nothing that its meaning goes awry. 'Language is satisfied with the opposition between something and nothing' (Saussure).[36]

36. *Course in General Linguistics*, revised edition (Duckworth, London 1983), p. 86.

No need of a '*virus ex machina*'. The bug is the product, quite simply, of the hyper-sensitivity of machines to final conditions. And our bug, our existential bug, is the product of hypersensitivity to the ideal living conditions provided for us.

Time's double arrow. The Big Bang and the Big Crunch are triggered simultane-ously, the end begins at the same time as the beginning. Things begin to disappear the very moment they begin to appear. The two dimensions intersect at every moment, and every instant is a site where the two arrows cross.

The illusion of a final development, like the illusion of horizontal lines. Illusion of the end. No irreversible point in time. Like a wind blowing in all directions at once, things go both from their beginning to their end and from their end to their beginning.

The Big Crunch is no longer the final outcome or the negative of the Big Bang. It has its own independent course and its own power, just as Evil has against Good in Christianity's fundamental heresy, Manichaeism.

Apoptosis. As soon as a cell is born, it begins to die. Not that it wears itself out and dies, as it were, of old age. No, as soon as it is born and its life programme begins, the opposite programme is automatically triggered too: the programme of its death. And, indeed, if something goes wrong with that programming of death, the cell will live indefinitely and develop to infinity.

These two powers are combined in everything, like centrifugal force and the force of inertia, like gravity and anti-gravity.

Can a flame illuminated by another flame also cast a shadow on a wall?

With celebrity, as with sexuality, there remains only the nostalgia for the time when these things were important (often in relation to each other). But the nostalgia for sex is itself still aphrodisiac. Or is it, rather, that sexuality is only ever nostalgic?

As far as I can remember, I have never been unhappy. Impossible to be unhappy – a congenital infirmity. This is a worse curse, a worse misfortune, than any other. It is like being blind from birth. They talk to you about a sighted world for which you have no evidence. They speak to you about a world of misfortune of which you have no deep sense.

We were in the twenty-first century long before the year 2000. Hence the prediction that the year 2000 would not take place. On the other hand, once the 2000 date was passed, we realized that we are still desperately in the twentieth century, if not indeed the nineteenth. This is perhaps one of the effects of the other arrow of time: as we drive on towards an ulterior state, we are at the same time charging in the other direction, towards a future anterior.

When you think that birds came from dinosaurs, you wonder what a similar fabulous transformation would do with the human race, and with mammals in general? Can one imagine anything as different from humans and mammals as the swallow is from the tyrannosaurus?

From west to east – this year end's hurricane followed exactly the same path as the solar eclipse last summer. The 'path of totality' became the 'path of nihility'[37].

When you follow the same path as the hurricane, at the same speed, from west to east, at over a hundred miles an hour in the train, you have the impression of being the hurricane itself.

He put all his objects through a lie detector. And what do you think happened? They all admitted they had lied about their functions.

He put reality and truth themselves through the lie detector. And they admitted they had never believed in those things.

Lastly, he put the lie detector itself through the lie detector. And it was like Malkovich short-circuiting himself: now, all was lies.

All our current media concerns have in French the suffix '-aire': *identitaire* (issues of identity), *sanitaire* (health concerns), *sécuritaire* ('law and order'), *humanitaire* (humanitarianism). The whole lot being *publicitaire* (promotional). There is in this suffix something which quite aptly characterizes our culture as the *funérarium*[38] of received ideas and single-track thinking.

Extraordinary scene in the film *Being John Malkovich*, when Malkovich himself gets into his own skin and, identifying with himself, engenders countless metastases

37. 'Path of nihility' in English in the original.
38. The place where guests foregather before the funeral service.

of Malkovich. The short circuit produces a kind of gigantic feedback, which we might term the 'Malkovich effect'.

They say TV programmes sell (books). And selling encourages reading, and reading is good for culture, etc. In the case of advertising, there is this same autosuggestion in spiral form: advertising sells, selling encourages consumption, and consumption gives pleasure.

The thunderous arrival of the year 2000 saw people taking a rain check on the event, keeping a low profile. Ultimately, the year 2000 was just bluff. Even the Big Bug didn't happen. A mix of satisfaction and deep disappointment at the catastrophe's failure to occur.

But wasn't the year 1000 also ultimately a mystification? A retrospective one: the great terror of the year 1000 was invented retrospectively, whereas we invented the terror of the year 2000 ahead of time.

The territory, the body, the real and this table have not disappeared physically, they have disappeared metaphysically.

In the past, catharsis was the purification of the passions by fire. Today it is their liquidation by flow.

Happy memories have become so only by the operation of memory. Standing in front of all these marvellous things, I have no imagination of what I am seeing. It is as though I were lodged deep inside my own eye, all consciousness snuffed out, watching them pass by from a great distance through its vitreous humour, its veil of boredom and *déjà-vu*.

The whole of the real is there, present. Sky, women, sun. And it is impossible to move to the act of representation.

The immense hubbub or brainwashing by which meaning and the real flow out in an endless haemorrhage. 'He saw the growing triumph of advancing tolerance – universal education, universal suffrage, majority rights, women's rights, children's rights, criminals' rights, unity of the different races, social security, public health, the right to justice – the struggle over three revolutionary centuries crowned with success, while the feudal shackles of church and family crumbled away, what had been aristocratic privileges spread widely to the population and were democratized, particularly the privileges of libido, the right to lose one's inhibitions, to be spontaneous, to urinate, defecate, belch, to mate in any position, in a threesome or foursome, polymorphously, to attain nobility through being natural, to be primitive, to combine ingenuity in leisure and the lustful pursuits of Versailles with erotic ease beneath the hibiscus trees of Samoa. A dark romanticism was taking shape today. With racism, all those strange erotic doctrines, exoticism and local colour having disintegrated, the masses had inherited all these things in an advanced state of degeneration, forming from them a certain idea of the evil of being white and the redemptive power of being black. . . .'

Current events are an incurable illness.

La Villa Palagonia, Palermo.

Surrounded by monsters, gnomes and misshapen figures formed in the image of the Duke of Palagonia who built it and who, being himself deformed and misshapen, to rectify fate's cruel disfavour cunningly covered all the rooms, including the ceilings, with convex or concave mirrors so that everyone appeared deformed or misshapen. This included his wife, who was very beautiful, but whom he could not bear to see pride herself on the fact. So he posted up the following words in the vestibule of the great hall (the residence itself is built in spiral form):

> *Specchiati in quelli cristalli*
> *e nell'istessa*
> *magnificenza singular*
> *contempla*
> *di fralezza mortale*
> *l'immago espressa.*

> Regard yourself in these crystals
> And in this same
> Singular magnificence
> Contemplate
> The express image
> Of a mortal fragility.

However, the Duke of Palagonia was himself mystified by his perverse imagination. For if the image underscores the mortal fragility of all things – and, particularly, of beauty – it merely *presents it to vision*. It *is not* that fragility, and it even protects us from it. If death is present in the image, it cannot at the same time be present in the imagination. In the end, the crystal absorbs death, the mirrors absorb monstrosity, and the image absorbs all real passions and transfigures their agony (*agonia* rhyming so well with Palagonia).

If the image is the presence of death, then there is no imagining of death.

If time is the pure image of all things, then there is no imagining of time.

If the image is the rival of the real, and a successful rival, then there is no imagining of reality.

So neither the Villa Palagonia nor the Catacombs of the Cappuccini, with their hundreds of embalmed wraiths standing in their passages, provide us with a sense of death or a mortal fragility. They are simulacra, and they negotiate death by the spectacle of death, death in itself being unimaginable. The – always more or less funereal and melancholy – charm of the simulacrum is that it allows us not to choose between illusion and reality.

The farandole of monsters in the villa's gardens, and the villa itself, are surrounded today, deep in the suburbs of Palermo, by a much worse monstrosity: that of the concrete tower blocks and the frenzy of traffic, of modern sound and fury – the true seventh circle of hell, as Ceronetti would say; the upsurge of a technicity which has wiped from its imagination the very idea of Evil, the principle of Evil, and by comparison with which the space of the villa stands as a last initiatory remnant, preserving in its mirrors, though not for long, the silence of fragility.

True death, annihilation, extermination, is there outside. The pure product of modernity, which, better than any moral value, the spark of Evil still resists.

People who are blind from birth and have their sight 'restored', or people who have had cataract operations, are often left completely at a loss – in a state of helplessness which can even end in suicide. Traumatized by this immersion in an unknown world – it is as though asexual beings were suddenly made a present of sex: what would happen to them? What would become of animals if we opened up the dimension of language to them? What happens to the human being who suddenly has his freedom restored (the serfs of Russia rebelled in their day against emancipation, and freedom is no doubt still continuing to have its destabilizing effect on us)?

It is an extraordinary mistake to think that every new function, sense or dimension automatically brings added value. This is the same problem as the adding of movement, sound, 3D and colour to the image. And the same question arises with our entry into Virtual Reality. What effect will the opening up of this artificial dimension have on our entire species? Is it to be something like a sixth sense to us? Are we like people born blind who might now be said to have had our sight restored? Are we 'cured by the Virtual', digitally saved, intoxicated with all these new opportunities, but also thrown into helpless turmoil by the opening up of a fourth dimension as alien to us as language might be to animals?

Rather than being miraculously cured of our ills, are we not rather like the *Énervés de Jumièges* – tendons cut, muscles limp and lifeless, drifting off on the raft of the Medusa, on the terminals of our liquid-crystal screens?[39]

'There isn't a woman in the world whose possession would be more precious than the truth she reveals to you by making you suffer.'

But what is this marvellous truth?

That possession is an illusion, and that suffering itself is useless? Isn't the truth, rather, that of a promise never kept, never lived up to? The truth is that woman has nothing more to offer you than possession, unless it be denial of that possession: denying herself to you as the truth denies itself to you. The revelation, then, is that possessing the truth, like possessing a woman, is an illusion, and that the world is definitively the work of Evil and the site of scandal. It is, in a word, the revelation of the nonexistence of God.

Yet the absence of truth, if it were revealed to us, would be more precious even than truth. Do we have to suffer to get to this? Every truth revealed by suffering is a mystification. Woman is a mystification. God is a mystification. This very

39. The legend of the *Énervés de Jumièges* was probably invented in the eleventh century. It relates how the sons of Clovis II were punished by *énervation* for leading an uprising against their mother, Bathilde, while their father was away at the Crusades. They are said to have been placed on a raft, which drifted down the Seine to Gemeticus (Jumièges), where the abbot Filibert took them into his abbey as monks.

COOL MEMORIES IV: 1995-2000

proposition is a mystification. It is a thing of beauty only in its literalness, in its impenetrable meaning, and because there is no more truth to it than that of which it speaks.

'This is the desperate time when, to act aright, you must lay down your life' (Françoise de Cézelli to the consuls of Narbonne – August 1582).